Of Love

& Bubbles

IGNITE YOUR LOVE

LET PASSION FUEL YOUR MARRIAGE

AND SET YOUR HEARTS ON FIRE!

DARES OLSON

Published By: DNP Presents

Library of Congress Cataloging-in-Publication Data has been applied for

ISBN: 979-8-9999454-2-6

PRINTED IN THE UNITED STATES OF AMERICA

Foreword

Few books about marriage have made as much of an impact on me as Of Love and Bubbles by Dares Olson. Without hesitation, I consider it one of the most insightful and helpful marriage books I have encountered.

Dares tackles topics that many authors shy away from. He writes with honesty about the intimate details of marriage—both in the bedroom and in daily life. Rather than glossing over difficult issues or remaining at the surface, he approaches marriage with courage, clarity, and depth, providing insight that is both refreshing and necessary.

While this is a faith-based book, it is not limited to people of faith alone. The principles shared here are grounded in truth, wisdom, and intentional love—values that speak to the human heart regardless of where someone is on their spiritual journey. God is present throughout this book, not in a forced or heavy-handed way, but as a steady foundation for commitment, healing, and growth.

As I read this book, I found myself thinking about marriage like a jigsaw puzzle. Each piece matters, and when one is missing or out of place, the whole picture is incomplete. This book helps readers identify the pieces that anyone struggling in their marriage needs. *Of Love and*

Bubbles highlights the gaps and the work that needs to be done.

What makes this book stand out is that Dares doesn't just point out what's wrong. He gives practical tools, showing how to address and work through issues and stay committed along the way. This isn't a book about blame—it's about solutions, growth, and restoration.

There is a deep emotional current throughout these pages. This is a book that invites honesty and reflection. It challenges the reader while also offering hope. It carries transformative power—the kind that can shift perspective, heal wounds, and strengthen commitment.

I believe every couple should read this book. Whether you are preparing for marriage, newly married, married for many years, or someone who has experienced divorce and is considering remarriage, this book is relevant and important. It meets couples where they are and gives them tools to move forward with intention and wisdom.

Of Love and Bubbles is also perfect as a study guide. It works well for group discussions, marriage mentoring, and teaching. I can see it being used in seminars, counseling, and churches everywhere.

This book will make a real difference for couples everywhere. It speaks with honesty, compassion, and courage—offering practical ways to understand marriage and build something lasting. **Dares Olson** has given readers a true gift, and I'm glad to recommend it.

BLESSINGS,
Dr Pamela Henkel
https://linktr.ee/Purposewithpamela

Table of Contents

Introduction

I want you to know right off the bat, that this book is about your marriage relationship, and it focuses on three key elements... passion, sex, and of course, bubbles.

I wrote this book because, for many years, much of the Church has avoided talking about or being involved in certain topics it deemed inappropriate. Sex and sexuality, even within the context of marriage, are very high on that list.

Most likely, the thinking is, we have a more eternal purpose here on earth and are supposed to focus on bringing light into the darkness. With that, it's understandable why we would not bother wasting our time dealing with things we consider to be inconsequential to that purpose. Unfortunately, we created a problem. By removing ourselves from these discussions the way we did, we've almost completely lost our voice of influence in that very area. Our silence has given free rein to the spirit of the world, which has been running with it for a very long time. Now, sex has become so perverted and so far out of focus that people don't even know if they are male or female anymore.

To make it worse, the Church has fallen prey to many of the same perversions spilled out by that spirit. Here in the body of Christ, our understanding of love and marriage has been so influenced by the world that we now have just as high, and in some cases, higher divorce rates than nonbelievers do. And we're supposed to be the light! We're supposed to be the ones showing them how it's done.

If you are like me, you can't help but ask yourself, **"Why? What happened?"**

Well, it makes sense that if the church doesn't talk about or deal with things the world is interested in, then the world will seek those who do. And thus, the spirit of the world has gladly stepped in to recreate one of God's most holy institutions. Marriage has become more about fulfilling selfish desire than giving selfless love... and it has happened with very little resistance from the Church.

So here we are. In this time where spiritual battles continue to increase against our society and most specifically our marriages, we have this opportunity to take back what the spirit of the world has been perverting all these years.

I have written this book because I believe God has asked me to be a voice of reality and truth. I believe it is time for us to face the facts and deal with sex for what God actually designed it to be: pure, passionate, undefiled, and rooted in wholeness.

This book is most specifically written to you, men and women who are living within the Biblical structure of marriage. It is all about highlighting some essential elements of your lives together that work toward building oneness between you. The more unified you are, the harder you will be to separate.

It's the kind of unity that doesn't happen by simply agreeing with each other. It happens when you are both committed to a common set of guidelines, with common goals. Having this **'like'** purpose allows you to move and flow as one, even if you don't agree on every little thing. Hopefully, the following thoughts and ideas will help you identify some common guidelines for your marriage, because where there is unity, there is strength.

Ultimately, I pray these words will help you men understand your wives a little better. That you would learn a little more about why you are the way you are. Even more importantly, I pray they help you articulate those things to your wives in a much more meaningful way.

Likewise, I also pray these words will help you ladies understand your husbands a little better. That you would learn a little more about why you are the way you are. Even more importantly, I pray they help you articulate those things to your husband in a much more meaningful way.

I also pray this little book will light you on fire... fire enough to save your marriage. I pray you will see the power of your passion and make it as important to you as it was to God when He formed you with it.

With that in mind, please maintain a sense of perspective. We're not here to giggle at body parts or share each other's fantasies. This subject matter is very natural and very real, so let's treat it that way.

In addition, please know this material is not intended to sound like the one great magical elixir that will fix whatever ails your marriage. Most likely, there will be more to consider than what I am presenting here. I am merely giving you things that I believe will help stabilize your foundation as a couple. The rest will be between you and God.

Finally, I'm writing from a position of much exposure and experience. I was born again at the age of 5 and grew up in a pastor's home. I have served the Lord and worked in some form of ministry my whole life. With that, my wife and I have been married since 1986, and I would describe our relationship much like a trip through the Rocky Mountains. Amidst the breathtaking views and heart-pounding thrills, we have also been to the brink of destruction several times over. I mean, it's been to that point where one more word, one more gesture, and we're done. With Holy Spirit's enlightenment, I've learned firsthand how I've messed up to the point of total failure, but then also how to come back from that imminent demise and be restored into relational wholeness. Our highs have been very high, but our lows have been... well... I'm thankful God is so long-suffering and merciful. My wife and I have proven, just like the statistics are telling us, that just because you are a Christian doesn't mean you know how to do marriage and relationships well. Just because you love God doesn't mean your marriage is guaranteed to last.

Adding to that, I have also lived in a lot of different places and been a part of a lot of different churches and ministries over the years. I have witnessed the success and failure in the marriages of countless different people I have seen and/or known. With Holy Spirit as my personal tutor, I've been able to learn a lot from having Him explain to me what I was witnessing or experiencing personally. These many years of 'enlightened experience' have brought me to where I am now, with what I believe to be a perspective that may be a little different from what you are used to, yet rich in wisdom and practical application.

Ultimately, though, if you make it all the way to the end of this book and decide that you just don't agree with what I've written, no problem. I am not your God, so I'm fine with that. Though it may sound like I think I know it all sometimes, I humbly acknowledge I don't. I am not an expert in any one of your personal lives, so instead of getting too detailed, I have tried to stick to general truths so as to let God deal with any of the more intimate details, as He sees fit.

Please remember, Holy Spirit is our teacher, so as you work through these pages, read with an open heart. If you come across something new, different, or hard to swallow, at the very least, give Him a chance to hit it with a red light or green light in your heart. He is the one who knows what you really need, so do your best to forget about me and allow Him to take whichever words are necessary and make them relevant to you. Allow His voice to be the one you hear.

OK then, here we go! Passion is the driving force behind everything you do. Sex by God's design is an incredibly important part of your married life. And, of course, bubbles, ah, bubbles... Well, bubbles are what bubbles are.

Passion

*W*elcome to the foundation. I'm glad you could make it.

Even though we usually consider other aspects of our Christian lives as foundational to our existence, passion is a crucial anchoring point in living out who and what we are in Christ.

Still, I'm sure you have several scripture references running through your minds, bringing you to all sorts of verses that talk about *"faith, hope, and love ... but the greatest of these is **love**."* And how *"this is the victory that has overcome the world, our **faith**."* And how it's *"by **grace** you are saved through faith, not of works lest any man should boast."* And how you *"can do all things through **Christ** who strengthens you,"* just to name a few. (1 Corinthians 13:13, 1 John 5:4, Ephesians 2:8, Philippians 4:13)

Look. Let's be real. These are all true foundational scriptures, and their validity is undeniable. The words and ideas in this book are not intended to compete against or discredit any truth God has given us, but to hopefully bring even greater understanding as to how they work through our lives. We are here to explore passion, so come, let us reason together.

In the full context of Scripture, it's important to remember how effortlessly God's truth flows together with itself. Faith works with hope, hope works with love, love works with grace, and grace works with mercy, etc. So much so that sometimes it's hard to tell the difference between them because in various circumstances, more than one of them will look alike.

In other words, they all *"work together for the good to them that love the Lord."* (Romans 8:28)

What this means is that if something is a legitimate word or idea from God, it will work with and through all His other truths. It won't interrupt their flow because it complements them, rather than arguing against them. Through these coming pages, I pray that you will be able to see how the truth of passion and its foundational impact on your life and marriage flow seamlessly with the rest of Scripture.

Let me start by saying this. The word **'passion'** does not even show up in the King James Version of the Bible. It only appears once in the New King James, where it is used to depict the lustful desires of the flesh (Galatians 5:24). The passion in this book is neither nonexistent nor a fleshly desire. It is an energy, a power that joins with love to become a superpower. It'll change a person's heart from caring for a person to being driven to care for a person, from loving someone to being in love with that someone. Passion is an unstoppable force in the heart of God and man. It is the part of agape that compelled God to give His only begotten Son, from John 3:16.

In humans, when passion is aroused or woken up, we lose our ability to resist. It grabs our hearts so powerfully we can't say no. And don't think you're an exception to this rule because Jesus Himself could not even resist when it arose in Him. It's recorded in Matthew 14:13-14…*"When Jesus heard it, He departed from there by boat to a deserted place by Himself. But when the multitudes heard it, they followed Him on foot from the cities. And when Jesus went out He saw a great multitude; and He was moved with compassion for them and healed their sick."*

Jesus was told about his cousin, John the Baptist, being killed, so He left for a deserted place to be alone. It's pretty obvious here. He was isolating Himself to mourn the death of His cousin. But it says the people followed on foot to where He went, and when Jesus saw them, He was moved with compassion and healed them.

Did you see that? Passion moved Him. When passion for the people arose in Jesus' heart, He couldn't say no. He was powerless to resist, even though He was mourning the unjust death of a person very special to Him.

That's why when you are dating someone, even though you may feel like you've got it all under control, you need to pay heed. This is a fire you don't want to start because if you do, you will get burned. It's supposed to burn you because that's how passion works.

The flip side is the reason I wrote this book. If you are married, stoking the fires of passion is the most certain path to a thriving marriage. You want it to burn and melt your hearts together. It's supposed to make you so crazy in love that trying to split you up becomes a hopeless endeavor. It'll even turn you into one of those cute old couples who hold hands as they walk in the park and whose eyes still sparkle when they look at each other.

To help you understand this concept of passion better, think of it as a descriptor of the word love. There is love, and then there is passionate love. Whenever you see a reference to God's love for people, it is agape. The thing that separates agape love from the way humans typically love each other is the infusion of passion. Agape love is passionate love. Therefore, we can consider the word **'passion'** and the phrase **'passionate love'** as interchangeable.

This is powerful because God's passionate love for you is why He can see you as perfect despite the way you behave. It's why all His thoughts of you are *"thoughts of peace and not evil to give you a future and a hope"* (Jeremiah 29:11). It's also why He was willing to give up His very best, Jesus, so He and we could grow closer together. He desires to spend more time together throughout eternity... eternity folks!

That's a long time together. No love of Earth will ever last that long. God's love is a **passionate love**. It's worth studying.

So, even though you may not see the word **'passion'** in the Bible, its presence is there. It's everywhere, and it started at the very beginning. The reason God created man was that passion requires a relationship. It requires someone else. He was not simply seeking a pet. His whole creation was about having a companion who would be willing to receive and then reciprocate His love. This way, they could grow close enough to never fall away from each other... forever and ever. In other words, so nothing, not even death, could ever separate them.

"For I am persuaded that neither death nor life, nor angels nor principalities nor powers, nor things present nor things to come, nor height nor depth, nor any other created thing, shall be able to separate us from the (passionate) *love of God which is in Christ Jesus our Lord."* (Romans 8:38-39 with the word passionate added in.).

With that being said, let's look at where we see this passion first show itself in direct relation to man. We will need to go back to the beginning, to when we were created, so take a look at Genesis 1:26... *"Then God said, Let us make man in Our image, according to Our likeness;"*

This verse hits me a certain way. Here, God is running through all the days of creation and giving account for the different things He was making and when He was making them. Then, out of the blue, He says this.

I get the impression, and please bear with me, that it's as if God were running through a checklist of the things necessary to make an earth. He knew what needed to be done and was doing it straight off the recipe card. Then He got to the man part and totally interrupted the regularly scheduled programming to bring this special announcement.

"Hey, Boys! We're going to make man a little different. We're going to make him in our image and after our likeness."

Clearly, there was agreement because verse 27 says they actually did what He said. This becomes the first time we see, as indicated from Genesis 2:7, that God physically formed something first and then breathed His own breath into it.

At that moment, we became the new and improved, most highly advanced version of any creature He had made up to that point. God, so it would seem, was not completely satisfied with just anything as a legitimate companion, so He made man, and made him differently.

It's pretty clear to see that the improvements had to do with creating man to be a spirit being in a physical form, as opposed to everything else that was a physical body with a soul. The element that facilitated this change, the thing that made the difference, was God's very own breath being the source of man's life.

We are given an image of something similar to this in Ezekiel 37:1-14. The hand of the Lord takes Ezekiel out to a valley filled with dry bones. He tells him to prophesy to the bones, which he does, and all the bones came together to form a bunch of dead bodies lying out in the desert. It wasn't until Ezekiel did step number two and prophesied to the breath that the wind blew life into the bodies, and they were able to stand up to be what God made them to be, and do what God made them to do.

I always thought it was odd how God made Ezekiel prophesy twice in order to get the dry bones to live. Then this idea hit me. In order for man to be a comparable companion to God, he would need to be able to choose whether or not he wanted to love God back. The only way for this to be possible would be for man to have a free will of his own.

So, in that light, it totally makes sense why Holy Spirit didn't do all of the reforming of the dry bones and breathing them back to life in one big step. It's like He is accentuating the fact that man, the one creature with the will to choose, is a two-part process. First, you form him out of the dust of the earth. Then you breathe Spirit life into him to make him alive. It's the union between the physical realm and the spiritual realm. The breath, or life of God, is the difference. It's that breath that gives people the will to choose and establishes man's heart as the true connecting point, a portal, if you will, between the spirit and the physical.

Clearly, with God, the companionship He needed and was working toward couldn't be provided by just anything. If so, He could have picked out any one of the animals He had already made, given it a little intelligence, and called it good. But God needed more than intelligence. He was not only looking for a companion that He could love, but also one that could choose to love Him back with the same kind of heart. This means the companion He created needed to be equivalent, or if you will, compatible with God Himself. Well, the only way for that to happen would be for God to put a piece of Himself in that companion. His willingness to do that very thing brings us to the true key element of this whole event. The driving force behind God's pursuit of a companion was His need for an equivalent relationship.

In a relationship, love, interest, emotion, and support can flow freely between each person involved. It's in a relationship where the connections between us take place. It's within the borders of a relationship that passion is ignited and fueled. Only through a relationship would this

God of all-consuming love be able to truly connect with that which He had made.

For this reason, even today, if you are a Christian, you could say your number one priority in life is to feed and foster your relationship with God. You might think it would be God Himself or accomplishing every task He lays out for you to do, but that's not quite it. God didn't make man because He wanted someone to focus on Him. And He didn't make man because He wanted someone to mindlessly do everything He said. God made man because He **wanted**, because He **needed** companionship. To Him, it's about the relationship more than anything else. God wants you to treat your relationship with Him like your personal Garden of Eden. And like He charged Adam, He wants you to **"Keep it,"** which means, keep it alive. Keep it healthy and vibrant. Keep it free from threats. Keep it filled with life and passion.

Now I understand this may sound a little odd, or even a touch sacrilegious to some of you. Remember, though, we are humans functioning under a sinful nature while relating to a perfect, pure, and holy God. As amazing as it would be to live a perfect spiritual life, we all still abide in a physical body that dwells in an imperfect physical world. The inherent shortcomings and imperfections of our physical humanity affect how we relate to such a powerful and passionate God.

Because of this, when we place our total focus purely on God, our nature cannot help but notice how tiny and insignificant we seem to be. We can't keep pace when compared to this All-Glorious Lord of Power and Might Who Reigns in Holy Righteousness Through Life and Eternity. We also see how nothing around us ever measures up to the wonder and glory God brings. Knowing we are stuck here in this lowly life, mired in physical imperfection, it gets way too easy to dwell on how unattainable it is for us to ever be like Him. Our human nature binds us to a mindset founded in guilt and insignificance. I've seen it too many times where people have hopelessly given up and walked away from their faith, stating that the idea of Christianity and living holy is an impossible dream.

Conversely, if we only focus on His will, due to this same nature, we inevitably end up thinking our righteousness, our place in the Kingdom, is dependent on whether or not we do what we are supposed to do. It's almost like clockwork. If we perform properly, everything will be all right. If we don't perform properly, it won't. Even though our spirit and mind may know better, our human nature can't help dwelling on how big a failure we are.

Mankind clearly needs a buffer. We need something that allows us to look to God and meditate on His will without falling to the weakness of human nature. Enter the relationship. Relationship allows us to connect with God. It facilitates our ability to love and be loved, to function with God free of the guilt and shame that would typically bog us down. Interestingly enough, people in a strong and healthy relationship with God are able to function beyond the inherent weaknesses of their humanity. In their lives, their first and foremost priority is to be keepers of their relationship with God, and through it, they are able to live with Him on His side of Adam's sin.

In other words, prioritizing the relationship opens up a completely different dynamic between God and us. The ultimate result ends up having a deeper love and stronger commitment to Him than what was there before. The magic ingredient, the reason this happens, is the focus of this chapter. It is passion. Relationships are passion's domain.

To bring perspective to it, passion keeps the garden alive. Passion keeps it healthy and vibrant. Passion keeps it free from threats. Passion keeps it filled with life... and fosters more passion. Passion is what deepens love and strengthens commitment.

Think about this. Take a stroll down memory lane back to when you were single and wondering who your future life partner might end up being. Do you remember how many people you saw around you in your life? How many of those did you think would be great to marry? How many of them were you genuinely passionate about? Notice that, unless your marriage was arranged, the person you ended up marrying was also the one with whom you invested the most relationally. You gave more to your relationship with that person than you did with anyone else, and consequently, that is the person you became the most passionate about. The world calls that **"falling in love,"** but it's not because of some magical, fairy tale moment in time. It's the product of a key human element functioning in all of us. The greater the investment in the relationship, the greater the passion that builds for that person.

Keep in mind, this principle is true of both romantic and platonic relationships. After all, Christ's passion for the people was not romantic but was equally as powerful as any romantic relationship ever was. Essentially, the way we humans prioritize other people in our lives is generally determined by the strength of the relationships we have with them. Because of this functional role, you can see how the relationship becomes an even higher priority than the actual person.

With that in mind, let's examine a few things a relationship provides for us, highlighting the reasons why it warrants such a high priority.

First, having a relationship with someone makes them a very real presence in your life, whether you can see them or not. God is an excellent example of this, of course, but think about your spouse. When the two of you are in different parts of the world, do you change who you are to behave like a wild and crazy single person again? Or do you still honor your relationship even though they can't see you? Did you only obey your parents when they were present? Have you ever been shopping and found something you knew your friend would like, so you bought it for them, even though they weren't with you?

See, even if those you care about are not physically with you, they remain a real presence in your life because of your relationship with them.

Secondly, it equalizes everyone who is a part of the relationship. It doesn't matter how popular or important anyone may be, regardless of their skin color, social status, age, or even their past. They are all equally valuable to that relationship.

This kind of thing is easy to see with famous people. When they are interacting with their fans, they are responding to people who are looking up at them. But when an old friend shows up, they talk to that person like a peer. The relationship makes them equal.

SIDE NOTE: Another thing that is quite common among people who are well-known is that they appreciate it when those around them don't get caught up in their titles or accomplishments. They prefer to be spoken to and treated like a normal, real person. Believe it or not, it is similar with God as well.

Please don't get flustered or upset by that. Yes, we enter His gates with thanksgiving and His courts with praise, but once you get inside, it's time to be real. That's when the robes come off, the crowns get hung on their peg, and it's time just to be yourself and let Him just be Himself as you walk together in the cool of the day. It's the companionship that God seeks.

Thirdly, relationships create a secure environment where their participants can dwell with each other in an atmosphere of love and acceptance, even if they mess up.

Ultimately, the relationship affects the value different people hold in your life. Therefore, the more effort you make to develop your relationship with a person, the more valuable that person will become to you.

Feeding and fostering your relationship with God has the same effect. You end up strengthening your commitment to Him. You also become much more attuned to His heart. You'll find yourself intentionally listening to and learning about His likes and dislikes, dreams and heartbreaks. You want to treat Him right, so you find out the things that make Him tick. You end up doing everything you can to ensure your relationship is healthy and strong, because that is where you connect with Him.

Again, I know this may sound a little strange, given that we are talking about God here, but it's true. Think about this. He is the one who loved us first and gave His son to save us hundreds of years before we were born. He has expressed His desire for our relationship with Him to be stronger long before we even had the chance to choose.

With all that in consideration, I'd like to bring up an important factor involved in strong, healthy relationships. The strength of your marriage has never been determined by the amount of desire you have to make it stronger. It is, however, impacted by how much you trust each other and how willing you are to trust each other more.

Like so many things in marriage, this trust goes both ways. Meaning, the level of trust you have in your spouse is only half the story. It also matters equally how much your spouse trusts you. Not only do you choose to trust, even when things are uncomfortable for you, but you also work to present your spouse with someone who can be trusted.

It's the same for your relationship with God. It's not only about how much you trust Him but also how much He can trust you. By loving unconditionally and giving His very best, He has demonstrated His passionate desire to have a relationship with each and every one of us. Unfortunately, not all those individual relationships will be the same, because the strength of each one will be directly impacted by how much that person and God can trust each other.

Through this relationship, we grow in our trust of Him and also give Him someone He can trust in return. This is quite important because even though we are equivalent or peer-level with Him within the context of our relationship, positionally, He remains the King of Kings and Lord of Lords. This fact exposes a couple of nuggets about God and life.

First, the anointing for success over any people group lies in the heart of their king (God's established leader), not in what the king will allow. This is because there will be things a king allows due to his love for his people, but those permissions are not where the anointing for success is. That anointing lies in the actual desires of the king's heart.

In other words, if you want to experience breakthrough anointing for peace, healing, victory over sin, sickness, and disease, etc., for you and your people, then you need to find out where the King's heart is. What does He like? What does He not like? How does He feel about the things you face and do as a people? When you find those things out and set them as your parameters to live by, an anointing is released over you that no enemy, be it man or spirit, can stop.

Many of us misinterpret God's willingness to let us do as we please as His blessing on us. But that's not what it is at all. His true blessing comes from the things He has in His heart. Our Father loves us enough to let us stretch our wings and express ourselves a little bit. And He's very patient with us as we get these things out of our systems. During those times, though, we need to understand that the river of God doesn't freely flow in our lives until we line ourselves up with His will, His desires. Functioning within His permission to do our own will doesn't cut it.

Take note, because if you are willing, you can save yourself a lot of time and effort throughout your life by forgoing the realm of what the King allows. Instead, put in the effort to find out where His heart is and live from that place. It matters because that is what makes you somebody He can trust. Be to God what David's mighty men were to him. They committed their lives to fulfilling the heart of their king. They were so good at it, they knew what to do even before David could give them a command. Here's an example from 2 Samuel 23:13-17..."*Then three of the thirty chief men went down at harvest time and came to David at the cave of Adullam. And the troop of Philistines encamped in the Valley of Rephaim. David was then in the stronghold, and the garrison of the Philistines was then in Bethlehem. And David said with longing, "Oh, that someone would give me a drink of the water from the well of Bethlehem, which is by the gate." So the three mighty men broke through the camp of the Philistines, drew water from the well of Bethlehem that was by the gate, and took it and brought it to David. Nevertheless he would not drink it, but poured it out to the Lord and he said, "Far be it from me, O Lord, that I should do this! Is this not the blood of the men who went in jeopardy of their lives?" Therefore he would not drink it. These things were done by the three mighty men."*

This kind of commitment to their king can only come through relationship. These men saw through David's imperfections and straight to his heart. Through their understanding of their king, they were willing to do anything for him, whether he asked them to do it or not. And in response, David trusted them implicitly.

This brings us to the second nugget of truth about God and life. The most influential person in a kingdom is not the king. It is the person whom the king trusts.

Just as with David, this kind of trust can only develop when a person consistently proves they will live by the king's convictions, even when the king is not present.

Take a moment to self-search and ask yourself, **"Can my King trust me?"** The answer to this question seems to be clearest in the most controversial areas of Christian life. These are the areas that don't have a specific verse or verses telling us in black-and-white whether something is OK or not OK for us Christians to do. They are things like smoking cigarettes, getting tattoos, wearing revealing clothing because it's in style, drinking alcohol, using swear words in our vocabulary, getting a bunch of piercings, entertaining ourselves with shows and movies that are filled with fear, humanistic ideals, or an outright glorification of sin, etc. It also shows in the way we conduct ourselves with our parents, our pastor, our principal, our police officers, president, or anyone else whom God has established as an authority in our lives.

Look. We already know our loving and patient King will accept us and not reject us if we participate in these kinds of activities, but where is His heart? Though He would allow it, how does He feel about these kinds of things in His heart, especially as it pertains to the kids in His family?

Any wise king only trusts those with whom he has a strong relationship. This is good to know because it's impossible to have a strong relationship with your King if you are not willing to go beyond the black-and-white letter of the law and get to know His heart. The children of Israel struggled getting past the commandments. They wanted God just to tell them everything they could and couldn't do. Moses was the only one willing to be responsible for choosing what he did or didn't do based upon what he found in the Heart of his King. Consequently, Moses was the only one of the bunch who knew Him for more than His acts. Moses knew God's ways because he knew God's heart, and God trusted him.

Consequently, this is what God intended when He created man in the way He did. He needed a companion who would let Him be their friend and be willing to be His friend. He needed someone who would be willing to lay their life down for His heart because that's what He was willing to do for them. He needed someone who would trust Him and be someone He could trust. He needed a companion who would stir up the agape He already had in His heart.

Like God, this is also the kind of companion man needs. Only a person who is of equivalent make-up, equivalent intelligence, and equivalent nature could stir us up inside. We are drawn to, compelled by, and passionate about that which is comparable to us because that's the only type of being that can fully reciprocate our love. God made this clear when He said He was going to make a **compatible** companion for Adam, not just a companion.

It was and is all about releasing passion. God needs a relationship to be passionate about. Man needs a relationship to be passionate about. Anything else is nothing more than a tool, or a toy. Even though some of them can do some great things for us, they ultimately don't relate the same. Passion makes the difference.

So, looking back at Adam, even though he could have walked and talked and grown old with any one of those amazing creatures God created for his earth, Adam still needed a peer-level human for a companion. He needed someone he could be passionate about, and boy was he! Even her title, Woman, is probably just as much Adam's first reaction to her as it was the literal definition of the word.

Look at how he responds in Genesis 2:23..."*This is now bone of my bones and flesh of my flesh; She shall be called Woman, because she was taken out of Man.*"

It worked, too. Just think about it. God told Adam, before Eve was on the scene, that if he ate the fruit from the tree of the knowledge of good and evil, he would die. Then she shows up. Now they're both out chilling in the garden when the serpent crashes the party and tricks Eve into eating the forbidden fruit. To Adam, the love of his life was just given the death sentence. In his mind, he was about to lose his soul mate forever.

Come on, people! This is the very first chick flick playing out right before our eyes!

So, Adam says, "*Eve. My darling Eve. I will not let you go! I cannot let you go! You are a part of me and the keeper of my heart. You are my very life, my breath, my dreams, my purpose. You are my evening and my morning star. You are my everything, Eve! I don't care about the gold or the glory, the life or the blessing if it's not with you. You are all I want, my love, my passion. I'll gladly give it all up for you because none of it means anything if you're not here with me! Eve, I love you!"*

And in one simple act of mindless passion, Adam ate the fruit too. He joined his fate to hers for all eternity and sold us all down the river at the same time.

You know, as utterly disappointed as God must have felt to have the soul mate He created for Himself pick the other girl, I can't help but think He may have also been a little proud of Adam. His design worked so well that Adam fell hard, helpless to resist his passionate drive to hold onto his love ... **no matter the cost.**

That Adam. He was such a romantic ...

Now then, here's another question. How high do you think our divorce rate would be if we were as passionate about our spouses as Adam was about his?

And compared to all those other more tangible endeavors in our lives, just how important do you think feeding and fostering our passion for each other is?

I say passion is the game changer. It's the driving force behind your very existence, spirit, soul, and physical body. You were created out of passion to be passionate. If you are not, you are the living dead.

Living your life without passion makes you like a zombie... trudging around and feeding on the living souls of whomever comes within your reach. And all the while, you fail to realize that you were not made to live that way.

Listen to these words from Dale Carnegie: *"Today is life - the only life you are sure of. Make the most of today. Get interested in something. Shake yourself awake. Develop a hobby. Let the winds of enthusiasm sweep through you. Live today with gusto."*

That sense of zeal and excitement, love and purpose, drives us forward. It's the reason we endure those mundane parts of our everyday lives and battle through those essence-stealing challenges life throws at us. It's a built-in function integrated into all our original programming to keep us from ever giving up. This should mean a great deal to us believers, because in our walk of faith, the only way we lose is by giving up. If you don't quit, you will win!

SIDE NOTE: Surprisingly enough, you will find that the people who tend to be the most passionate in life are people who live their lives in some form of service to other people. The principles of passion are true for married and single people. Only humans can be the compatible companions we need. Only humans can feed and foster our passion for life. When we get involved in human-helping activities, it opens the door for agape to flow through us. Since that is what passion is all about, living for these types of causes will fill you with more Zoe than any personal goal or desired treasure ever could.

If you are single and searching for your soul mate, your solution is simple yet complex. Quit searching for your perfect match and pursue your calling. God has a fantastic plan for your life, and it involves helping another person or persons. Give yourself to serving where God places you. Go assist in humanitarian works, take mission trips, and expand your personal horizons. Be that servant to man God made you to be.

As you do, you will be placing yourself right where God needs you to be. The more your attention falls away from you and your search for your soul mate to satisfy your needs and your desires, the more He can fill your heart with His love and purpose for others. Ultimately, when the time is right, God will bring your partner to you. He will make sure of it.

The thing is, when He does, you will be a whole lot more like the person your spouse is searching for as well. By feeding and fostering your passion through serving God and others, He shapes you and makes you into the very person your soul mate needs and wants, as well. Then, not only are they the answer to your prayers, but you are their dream come true as well.

It's as simple as you getting yourself out of your way.

OK, back on point. Focusing on the relationship so you can feed and foster passion is a critical consideration. It is one of the reasons why the discussion about sex is such a big deal. Coming up in Chapter 2, we're going to see how, at the very moment God separated female from male, passion and sex were instantaneously instituted into their relationship. He had it all set in place by forming their bodies in such a way that they could passionately reconnect as one again.

Passion was there then, is here now, and always will be the driving force that compels us to reconnect. God knew we would need this motivation, so He breathed His passionate love into us and then gave us to each other.

Passion, again, is the key.

In that, I'd like to point out something else to help validate what I am saying.

We all know God is love. This means He would have loved all the life He created on earth. But even though He loved them all, they were not all compatible companions. So, as we mentioned earlier, God makes man and makes him differently by breathing His spirit life into him. Now we have the ability to choose to love Him back.

This, of course, is the same element that makes our companion the one who fuels our passion as well. This is what puts the fire in our eyes and the jump in our step, too.

You see, unlike our pets who instinctively love and never hate or judge us, we humans contain the power to choose. Animals love in response to instinctive protocols in their brains. When you understand an animal's settings, you can pretty much get any one of its species to love you because it is based on instinct.

With humans, though, you can do everything the way you are supposed to do it with a person, and they can still choose not to respond favorably to you... simply because they don't want to.

Without this chosen reciprocation, everything about life, love, and companionship becomes nothing more than that new toy syndrome. You get a new toy. You're excited and passionate about it because of how amazing it is. Then you end up getting bored by reason of use. The magic of it wears off and it becomes just one more thing added to your collection of things.

The only way we could continue to love a choiceless object for any length of time is if that thing continues to provide some desired service for us, like a trusty old pick-up truck or pair of old slippers.

But if you throw a little reciprocation into the mix, now you're on to something. Reciprocated love is the secret to passion because it is the product of a person's choice. Quite obviously, a thing needs the ability to choose in order to love someone back.

Now this may sound a little strange, considering how God's kind of love gives, no matter how good, bad, or ugly the recipient may be. That's just what it does. It is completely disconnected from any requirement, and that is where things get good. With the complete lack of expectation, you can imagine what kind of internal response it renders when somebody stops, says **"Thank you,"** and then reciprocates your goodness in their own special way. Something goes off down inside. A fire ignites. Eyes begin to sparkle. Desire appears, and suddenly there is an intense drive to do even more for that person than before.

It's amazing because even though God's love doesn't expect or require anything in return, when we love Him back, it melts His heart. After all, He knows we're doing it by choice. We're not responding to Him because of His requirement, but because of our desire.

I think you all can understand just how much more meaningful it is when we know someone is expressing love to us purely because they want to love us. It melts us down to our core, just like it does with God.

Just in case you're still not sure, let me give you a non-romantic example of what I am talking about. Let's say you are a father with two daughters. They are similar in age, and you love them both very much. One day, you decide to bless them, so you take them to the mall and buy each one a new dress. On your way home, one of them is engaged in text conversations with her friends and internet searches on her phone. The other one can't stop looking at and talking to you about how pretty her new dress is, and how she can't wait to wear it.

When you get home, the phone girl grabs her stuff and says, *"Thanks, Dad. I love you,"* and then disappears to her room. The other one grabs her stuff and runs off without saying a word. A few minutes later, though, she emerges with her new dress on and her hair fixed up a little more than it was before. She comes in to where you are and says, *"Look, Daddy! What do you think? Isn't it pretty? Thank you so much! I love you, Daddy!"* Then she jumps up in your arms and gives you a big hug and kiss on the cheek, spins around a couple times, causing her dress to flair out, and then darts off to the kitchen to make you some of her special cookies.

Now you didn't buy them each a dress because you wanted them to love you more, or because you wanted cookies. You did it because you love them... period. They could have ignored entirely you the rest of the day, and you would not have minded because you didn't require anything in return for your goodness to them.

So, in this situation, which one of your two daughters are you going to be most motivated to bring back to the mall and bless again?

It's human nature, you see. We are made to respond very favorably to reciprocated love.

And if you did get the openly thankful daughter another dress, would it mean that you love your phone girl any less than this one? Absolutely not!

The thing is, by responding with a grateful heart and doing something special in return, this daughter set herself up to experience more of her father's love than her sister will. She is no better or more valuable than her sister is, but she is fueling and fostering her father's passionate love for her.

As a father of daughters myself, I can attest to this being true. When our little girls respond to us in this way, we are truly powerless to resist. We can't say no. We will find a way to bless our little lady again. And as odd as it may sound, it doesn't matter how it might make the other sister feel because it has nothing to do with her. It has everything to do with the one who chooses to love us back... and God is exactly like that with us.

Now apply this same principle to your married life, where romance and sexuality are involved. In this setting, you can crank up the volume and kick in the afterburners because things are about to jump to light speed! When true selfless romantic love is reciprocated, it erupts like a volcano down inside you. It is the high-octane fuel that powers your romantic passion. When you add sexual desire to the mix, you are now talking about an irresistible drive to reconnect, coupled with an irresistible power that binds you together. It drives you to become one and stay one.

This again is a big reason why we Christians must stop being afraid to talk about passion and sex in the context of marriage. The power of God that binds us together may be our love for Him on the spiritual side, but in the natural, it's our passionate love for each other.

When He says, *"What God has joined together, let no man put asunder!"* He doesn't just leave us hanging to try and figure out how to do that on our own. He gave us everything we needed to make it happen.

So then, taking this back to what we were looking at before, when God created the heavens and the earth, He did something that He had not done before. He made man by taking a piece of His self and using it to bring him to life. God did this because He knew He didn't just need a companion, but a companion He could be passionate about.

46

In other words, He needed someone who could choose to love Him back.

OK. Another reason why God needed a companion He could be passionate about is that as long as there is passion, love will flow. If His love is flowing, His power is being released.

In this, our relationship with God becomes a thoroughfare for His love to flow to us and through us into the earth. It gives Him legal presence in all things happening here, despite the prince of the power of the air working against it.

I don't think any of us would disagree that God's power needs to be released in all the earth. Because of this, we need to feed and foster our passion for Him. From that point on, it is one of those **'one step leads to another'** type scenarios. Passion drives our love for Him into action. This causes the love between us to grow. It opens the door wider for more of His love to flow back to us and through us. This reciprocation makes our passion for Him stronger, which drives our love to even more action. This causes the love between us to grow. And the cycle continues as it fosters and grows into perpetual motion.

It's all very simple, really. Passion is the key. Passion is power. It pushes us towards goals, breaks us free from addictions, and it'll even drive us to our knees. Passion is the driving force of life.

Think about what happens when you take some normal friendship-type love between people and mix a little passion (compassion) in with it? Suddenly, that love wakes up and becomes proactive. Suddenly, they must start doing things for each other. They're driven to help, protect, or care for the other person or persons way more than they ever did before.

It's even more profound between a man and a woman, romantically. Let them share a nice, mutually gratifying platonic friendship. Add a bit of passion to the mix, and the next thing you know, they can hardly keep their hands off each other. They're always together and always doing things for each other. Somehow, they went from simply loving each other as friends to falling mad-cap, crazy in love.

This isn't just true for us humans either. Passion is what takes God's love from being a passive truth to an active force, ministering life to everyone it touches.

We can take this another step further. Passion will not only affect how much you give and receive love individually, but it will determine how much of an impact you have on the overall world around you.

Listen to these words from revivalist John Wesley. *"Light yourself on fire with passion and people will come for miles to watch you burn."*

It's similar to what John 13:35 tells us… *"By this all will know that you are My disciples, if you have love for one another."*

The concept of this love here is passionate love. True love can be seen because it is driven to action. When true love is seen, other people want to be a part of it. They are drawn to it just like they're drawn to fire.

Jesus is our best example, but interestingly enough, not every person who was drawn to Jesus got saved or experienced a miracle. Yet, every single person who was drawn to Jesus was somehow affected by Him. He was a polarizing force who made you either love Him or hate Him, and you couldn't help yourself.

He was passionate about His Father, which explains why He fed and fostered His relationship with His Father as much as He did. He copied Him all the time and wanted to be just like Him. He even told us as much by letting us know that He says what His Father says and does what His Father does. In fact, we never see Jesus introduce Himself as Jesus, but rather almost always as the son of someone. Even more, the only time we see Jesus lose His temper was when He defended His Father's house. Jesus' passion for His Father fueled His love for us humans.

This happened because when you passionately love someone, an interesting phenomenon takes place. You begin to love what they love and hate what they hate. The desires of that person's heart become the guiding parameters of yours.

Why do you think it was such a big deal for us in this new covenant that the black-and-white commandments of God be taken off that which was rigid and written on the fleshly tablets of our hearts?

You see, in this new and improved covenant that is more about connecting hearts than abiding by rules, all the restrictions over God's free-flowing love have been removed. We are now unlimited in how, why, or when we express our love to God. If our hearts are in the right place, there are no rules.

Let me interpret what I just said. If your passion for God is the driving force behind your expression of love for Him, you have no limitations on how to do it.

This covenant we are in is driven by passion. It is all about opening the floodgates and letting His love flow. In that sense, it is safe to say a passionate life is a liberated life. Passion sets you free to live like Jesus lived, love like Jesus loved, and give like Jesus gave. It is the driving force for life.

♥ The Difference ♥

Well then. This seems like a good place to change directions slightly and clarify that love and passion are not the same thing. Love is the substance that contains God's **'zoe'** life for us. Passion is the power that makes it flow. This is why when we refer to passionate love, we are speaking of a love that has been empowered.

This concept may seem a bit foreign to you, but in dealing with it, please answer the following question. Have you ever met somebody who got divorced from someone they still loved? I have, more than once. I would venture to say it happens quite often.

In the same light, please answer this question. Have you ever met somebody who divorced someone they were passionately in love with?

Me neither. It just doesn't happen, except for perhaps some truly strange or precarious circumstance.

In the simplest form, this is the best way I could think of to say it. Essentially, for us humans, it's possible to love someone and not be passionate for them. If love and passion were the same thing, this would not be possible.

On the flip side, it is entirely impossible to be passionate about someone and not love them.

Of course, I'm not talking about a couple who come together for a one-night stand in a fit of **'passion'** and then go about their separate ways. That does not qualify as real passion even though our modern vernacular uses the word to describe their steamy encounter.

To further clarify, here is another way to see it, but using an element of nature. Electricity is partly defined as a flow of electrons. In electricity, the power that causes light to appear from a light bulb, or heat to appear on your stove, is called current. It is measured in Amps. For simplicity's sake, we'll say that amps are the amount of electrons that are flowing.

These amps don't just flow on their own, though. There is a force that pushes or drives them. This force is called Voltage. The higher the voltage, the greater the number of amps that can be pushed.

If one of these two elements is absent, there is no flow. Electricity will not be present. You could have enough amps available to light up the city of New York, but if you don't have any voltage to drive that current forward, you have nothing.

That is like the difference between love and passion. His love is equivalent to the amps that light the lamps in our hearts, cover our sin, and fill us with hope. But His passion is like the voltage that pushes that love into action. Passion is the driving force that compels His love to reach out to us, cover us, minister to us, and ultimately flow through us to bring His life into the world.

If there is no flow of electrons, there is no manifest power. If there is no flow of God's love, there is no manifest power.

You see. Electrically speaking, power is the result of Voltage and Amps working together. This is just like God's power. It is the product of His Passion and His Love working together to fill our lives and reach the world.

♥ *The Effect* ♥

Over these pages, we have looked at different characteristics and details about passion. I would like to take a moment to talk about some of the ways we are directly affected by passion when it shows up in our lives. Hopefully, this will help to tie a lot of this together.

First, let's identify that there is what I call Platonic passion, and then romantic passion.

Platonic passion is the passion inside of you that impacts your relationships with the people in your life, other than your spouse. It is all about sharing the love of God and building an atmosphere of peace and unity among all people (peace on earth, goodwill toward men).

Romantic passion is the passion inside of you that impacts your relationship with your spouse. It is all about drawing a married man and woman together and making them whole, or complete again, through their relationship. It helps them to flow and function as one complete person. Add Holy Spirit to the mix, and it's that three-fold chord that is not easily broken.

Many but not all the effects are the same for both types of passion, but the way they manifest can be monumentally different ... if you know what I mean.

In both cases, passion will change how you see a person or persons. Without even realizing it, you will find yourself thinking and seeing the positive aspects of those other people in your life. Even worse, it dulls your senses to their faults.

It's like this. If you want to see your wife the way God sees her, take her away and spend some time making steamy, hot, crazy, passionate love with her. Then, as the dust is settling, look at her. She looks like pure love and desire. Her faults may be present, but are entirely imperceptible. Your hearts are interwoven and irreversibly bonded together. Your eyes sparkle, and you feel an overwhelming sense that you can't get enough of her. She is perfect, and life is beautiful. It's as if you *"know the thoughts you think towards her, thoughts of good and not of evil, to give her a future and a hope,"* (borrowed from Jeremiah 29:11).

The reason for this is that when you are passionate, you are functioning like God functions. You will see like He sees, hear like He hears, and think like He thinks. Your approach to humanity, both platonic and romantic, takes on a whole different flow. You stop protecting yourself first because your attention is on them.

To get pure-to-plain about it, people you are not passionate about are people you don't care enough about to love this way. It happens to all of us. I often encounter people in life whom I don't know. I have no drive inside to know them. I don't care what they're doing or where they are going. I am entirely indifferent.

I even have relatives whom I genuinely love. But they live where they live, and I live where I live. They have their lives, and I have mine. When we get together, we enjoy love, laughs, and memories, but at the end of the day, when we go our separate ways, our general interest in each other goes with us until we meet again.

Look, I'm not saying this is good or bad. I'm just saying this is the way it tends to be. But those people or relatives whom I am passionate about are in a different category. They are essential parts of my daily, weekly, or monthly life, so I actively pursue activities and time with them.

Additionally, if people we are not passionate about irritate us or reveal any flaws, we tend to write them off. We are generally satisfied never to see them again. Whereas when we are in love, or if you will, driven by passion, we have this uncanny ability to look straight past a person's faults and right to the value they bring. It's as if we can only see how good the person is, instead of what a pain it is to deal with them.

As many of you know, it can be quite annoying to deal with people who are functioning this way. They don't want to listen to anything that isn't purely positive about the person they love.

Passion is the cause of it all. It affects your mind so much that it'll have you giving things like grace and mercy to people when they deserve judgment and punishment. It is what 1 Peter 4:8 means when it says, *"And above all things have fervent love for one another, for love will cover a multitude of sins."*

Living passionately will also cause you to live by a specific set of character traits known as the Fruits of the Spirit. Here they are from Galatians 5:22-23: *"But the fruit of the Spirit is love, joy, peace, longsuffering, kindness, goodness, faithfulness, gentleness, self-control. Against such there is no law."*

This can also be irritating to see sometimes. You get a person in your life who rubs you the wrong way. They annoy and bother you. Generally, like nobody else, they can make you hate ice cream, flowers, sunshine on a spring morning, and anything that makes life worth living. Then you see them interacting with that one person in their life they're passionate about, and they are the epitome of love and peace and joy and kindness and goodness and Just Shut Up Already!

This principle is true, though. We see it play out all around us, and most particularly within the confines of our marriages. Somehow, living passionately causes us to live like real Christians are meant to live, with the world and each other. Selah.

♥ *The TP* ♥

This is like dynamite right here. It is a small section, but it packs a massive punch.

You definitely do not want to attempt to live passionately without having enough TP to back you up.

Psalms 100:4 tells us that if we want to go visit God and spend some time with Him, we *"enter into His gates with Thanksgiving and into His courts with Praise"* ... **TP**.

The imagery here is easy to see. Gates are usually at the entrance to a property. Courts are generally near a door to the house.

A thankful heart is the key that unlocks the gate, allowing you to gain access to the landscape of God's heart. Praise is what gets you to and through the door.

We all have our ideas about why God is like this, why these requirements exist to get to His heart. The part I'd like you to notice is this. Your spouse was created in the image and after the likeness of this very God, who requires such things.

Do you think maybe, just maybe, the key to the gate and passage through the courts of your spouse's heart might be thankfulness and praise also?

Is it possible that focusing on the things you can be grateful for and expressing said thanks could cause a stirring in their heart? Could it realistically draw their affections toward you?

Is it also possible that by giving praise to them, you can compel them to open their heart's door and invite you to come in and commune?

You see, having a thankful heart is not just a key. It is **the** key to living a passionate life.

As powerful an impact thankfulness and praise may have on your spouse, or even all those other people you encounter in your life, the one most affected by it is you.

The key to the gate of your heart is thankfulness. Passage through the courts leading to the door of your heart is praise. But let me ask you a couple of all-important questions.

Just like with your physical house, who holds the key to your gate? Is it you or the visitor trying to get in?

And who controls access through your courts? Is it you or the visitor trying to get in?

You see, if you do not have a thankful heart, you will not be able to open your own gate to let anybody else in. It is a deception to think that your joy and fulfillment are contingent on other people because you are the one who holds the key to your own gate.

When you are thankful in your heart and can freely praise the good in others, you are more receptive to others being thankful for and praising you.

If you are not this way but focus more on protecting yourself from their obvious shortcomings, you will not be as open to receiving people or the love they may be trying to bring to you. You do what we call **'keeping people at a distance'**... or if you will, stopped at the gate.

The reality is, it doesn't matter what good or bad anybody says or does to you. It is only when you learn to be thankful for what you have, rather than being mad about what you don't, that you will be able to open the gate and allow passage through your courts.

Thankfulness is the key, and you hold the key.

Why is this important in this discussion about passion? It's simple, really. The trigger to passion, if you remember, is when somebody chooses to love you back.

If you are not thankful, not only will you not receive others' love, but you will not choose to love them back either... most specifically in a way that feeds the relationship. In other words, you are stopping the passion cycle right there at you.

Because of this, whether dealing with your spouse or with all those other people God has brought into your life, you never want to get caught without your TP.

Thankfulness and Praise help flush your system of all the negative stuff that builds up from everyday life with people. It keeps your heart clean and free from baggage. It fills your life with the sweet aroma of love and hope.

Otherwise, if you don't have your TP, life can really **stink**!

This is why it was so crucial for me to address thankfulness within the context of passion. Your ability to stir others up by being a loving benefit to their lives is directly connected to how thankful you are in your own heart. If you don't have it when you come to their gate, they will never let you in.

Conversely, your ability to be stirred by other people who are trying to be a loving benefit to your life is directly connected to how thankful you are in your own heart. If you don't have it, you will never let them in.

♥ Wrapping Things Up ♥

So then, I hope you can see that passion is not to be taken for granted. We cannot afford to let it take a back seat in our lives. God made us to be passionate people, and He made us to need somebody to be passionate about.

It's easy for us to lose sight of it because it is intangible, meaning we can't write it into a check to pay the light bill or cook it up for the kids to eat for dinner. But we must stay vigilant.

In the day and hour we live, we must make passion a priority. If necessary, we may need to revisit what we are doing in line with God's plan for our lives. His will contains a lot of passion mixed into it. Otherwise, we end up like the church in Revelation 2:1-5. Jesus acknowledges the good works they have done, but then in verse 4, *"Nevertheless I have this against you, that you have left your first love. Remember therefore from where you have fallen; repent and do the first works, or else I will come to you quickly and remove your lampstand from its place - unless you repent."*

In our life on earth, our **"first love"** is our relationship with God. It is the most important thing of all. If we lose our passion for Him, all our relationships suffer, and we end up losing our impact in the earth. We keep it strong by focusing on it, feeding and fostering it, and stirring up the passion in our hearts for Christ.

In our marriages, our **"first love"** is our relationship with each other. For us to survive through thick and thin till death do us part, we need to find a way to stay passionately in love. We feed and foster those fires so when trouble and circumstance wear us down, we don't walk away.

By focusing on the relationships, we align our hearts with the heart of the other person, thus ensuring the devil will not be able to break us apart from God or each other. We fan the flames of our passion and let it fuel our burning desire to be **one** again, to be whole and complete.

Passion is the key. Feed it. Foster it. Let it burn.

Ferdinand Foch, the French general who served as Supreme Allied Commander during the First World War, said it this way, *"The most powerful weapon on earth is the human soul on fire."*

Passion. It's as if God knew ...

Sex

"Oh Lord! Plug yer ears Ma! He's gonna infect yer brain!"

*M*y goodness. Sex!

Some of you may be giggling. Some of you may be shrieking in holy terror. Some of you are the epitome of apathy. Others of you may be staunchly unmovable and are otherwise sitting there wondering what this guy thinks he knows.

Either way, right here, right now, and no matter how you may be approaching it let's just put it all out on the table for the whole world to see. Sex. It's a thing. It's a very real thing.

There. Now that we have that established, please allow me to ask the following leading question as if you were thinking this thought.

Aside from the obvious purposes of reproduction and the pleasurable bonus of having a good time with your spouse, what else do we legitimately need to know?

It's an honest question, and in answering it, I would like to take our discussion beyond the typical ideas of pleasure or reproduction and look closer at reason. Let's check out perspective and investigate purpose. You know—all those incredibly arousing things that instantly pop into your mind when someone says something about sex.

You may not think so, but I believe this is going to be great! So here we go.

♥ *The Reason* ♥

Let's start talking about sex by going back to the beginning ... again. In this, please work with me, for I will surely paraphrase.

In the first chapter of the Bible and the very first verse, God created the Heavens and the Earth. Then, as stated earlier, through the rest of this chapter, we see a record of God creating and setting in place all the parts and pieces that go into the Earth, along with the systems that make it work.

Then we get to the part about man in verse 26 where God says, *"Let Us make man in Our image, according to Our likeness; ..."*

Then in verse 27, He does what He says. Here it is, along with a part of verse 28: *"So God created man in His own image; in the image of God He created him; male and female He created them. Then God blessed them, and God said to them, 'Be fruitful and multiply; fill the earth and subdue it; have dominion ...'"*

When you look closely here, you see God creating man and then giving him four things. These things are just as real today as they were back then.

Right off the bat, the very first thing God ever gave to man was **each other**. He took one, split that into two, and then gave them back to each other to be one again. That is how mankind, as we know it today, began. It was the beginning of male and female.

You can see it in verse 27. In the first part, it refers to man as only a him. But in the rest of the verse, you see how God gave that man someone besides just **"him"**. He had created a female to accompany the male and then set them up together.

It's significant to understand that this couple was the first institution of divine power God set up on the earth. This was His original plan for how He would fill the earth with His love and establish His will forever. It was one man with one woman, united by God and shamelessly naked.

Yes, I did say they were naked. It's right there in Genesis 2:25. There is a reason for it, so we will look a little deeper in a soon-to-come side note.

After giving them to each other, the next thing God gave man was the blessing. Essentially, He gave them everything they needed and would need to fulfill His desire for them on the earth.

Then, God gave them a job, or if you will, a purpose. With it, He instructed them to be fruitful and multiply, fill the earth. In this, He was establishing the concept of seedtime and harvest, otherwise known as the principle of sowing seed.

The last thing God gave to man here was the authority to do the job. In verse 28, He said, *"Subdue it, have dominion over the fish of the sea, over the birds of the air, and over every living thing that moves on the earth."*

This was the total package. He created them and brought them together. He blessed them, gave them a job, and then bestowed on them the authority to carry it out. God covered all the bases here.

This whole sequence is substantial because it shows how He is very willing to do His part to help you, and all His other couples function the way He designed you to function. God wants you to live your married life to the fullest, for good reason. One of which is because when you do, you bring glory to Him. For any creator, very little can bring greater joy than when the creation actually does what it was created to do. Married people are made to be an integral part of filling the earth with His love and life, simply by how they live as married people.

Not only that. Living your married life the way God designed it creates the kind of environment where the individuals involved can experience, in an everyday way, all the benefits and love God has in place for each person. God wants us to know He loves us, but not just because the Bible says He does. He wants us to know it because we experience it in a very real way, all the time.

SIDE NOTE: If you are like me, you believe that God inspired every scripture in the Bible and it is there because He wanted it there. It has a purpose. So, what would be the purpose of what God said in Genesis 2:25? "And they were both naked, the man and his wife, and were not ashamed."

I believe there is a little more here than what meets the eye, so let's take a closer look. This verse was written on the perfect side of marriage, before Adam's sin introduced a whole new set of circumstances to deal with. Since they had not messed up yet, they were functioning here the way God originally designed a married couple to function. In other words, this was doing it right.

Yes, you read that correctly. Getting naked together is a right thing to do (and all the men started shouting praises to the Lord.)

Before getting too excited, though, let's take a more objective approach. I believe there is some essential wisdom to be gained here that goes beyond our natural desires.

First, let's acknowledge the elephant in the room. It says the man and his WIFE! It doesn't say the man and his **'woman'**, or the man and his internet fascination, or even the man and the woman he was with. It says the man and his WIFE!

I've looked it up in several different translations of the Bible just for verification, and they all say the same thing. So, in God's eyes, the people who are cleared to be naked together and not be ashamed are a man with his wife.

Now then, another plain and simple application of this verse is almost as obvious as the first one. It says the two of them can be naked together and not be ashamed. This means that whenever you and your spouse are alone with each other (notice they were the only persons present), if you so choose, you can shed the clothes and enjoy being free-to-the-breeze in each other's presence with an assurance that neither God nor your spouse will make you feel ashamed or embarrassed for it.

Ladies, I acknowledge this can be tough because for many of you, a good bit of your self-confidence stems out of this very thing. You may feel like you have too many wobbly bits, or you're not shaped right, or your girly assets are too big or too small, which makes you feel less than acceptable when you are uncovered. Remember though. God didn't build you for you or your self-image. He fearfully and wonderfully built you for your husband, and he for you. In other words, you don't have to worry about whether you look well enough when you are completely exposed to your husband. Liking your naked little body is his job, not yours.

Notwithstanding, guys, though you may love seeing her that way, you must remember. She is your wife, not an inflatable toy who is only there for you to have fun with. So, *"dwell with her with understanding."* After all, *"Can two walk together unless they are agreed?"* (1 Peter 3:7 and Amos 3:3).

With the obvious out of the way in this verse, let's look a little deeper to see if something even more valuable is hiding beneath the surface.

The word **'ashamed'** is an emotion. It's a feeling. Some translations even say, *"they didn't feel shame"*.

This is a monumental discovery because here, at the very beginning of male and female's lives together, God made sure to identify how they were feeling. It's a big deal because even God seems to be acknowledging that how you both feel is an identifier, a factor in determining if you are doing marriage right.

I believe this is why. Now that the two of you have become one, the way you conduct yourself as a husband or wife will have a direct effect on how your spouse feels. Your behavior and their feelings are interconnected. This means you have a responsibility to God and to each other to do what you do and say what you say in a way that helps establish and maintain an environment free from shame. It solidifies the idea that has been thrown back and forth for many years. It's not what you say but how you're saying it. Or it's not what you do but how you're doing it.

This idea is like a litmus paper. If your marriage is healthy, both of you will feel loved, safe, secure, desired, needed, valued, fulfilled, etc. Sure, you may have breakdowns occasionally, but the established base emotional state of your marriage will be the like.

Now it's still true that we are not supposed to be led by our feelings. This rings true because to create and keep the right kind of shame-free environment this verse implies, you absolutely must be in control of your emotions. You cannot allow them to dictate how you give and receive communication from your spouse. As humans, our emotions play a significant role in our communication, but they cannot be in charge.

This is an area where having a good marriage is like being a good Christian. Both will require personal growth if you are given to let your feelings rule the school.

The last noteworthy aspect I notice in this verse is the word 'naked'. We've already covered the naked that refers to having no clothing on your body, but that is not its only meaning. It also represents transparency. We all need to be transparent. We also have an equivalent responsibility to allow our spouse to be transparent in front of us... key words here... without shame.

We all understand that not everything in life makes you happy. As an emotional creature, then, there will be times when you may be feeling down, depressed, or less than valuable. When this happens, you should be able to drop your guard to be vulnerable and real in your spouse's presence. This should be accompanied by a resolute confidence that they will not make you feel even more ashamed about your less-than-perfect state of being. And, of course, this sense of security should be mutual for both spouses.

Granted, this may not always be an easy thing to do, especially during those times of intense fellowship. But if you don't have room in your heart for your spouse to shamelessly feel and deal with the whole spectrum of human emotion, then you end up joining everything else on the list of things that are ruining their day. You do have to choose whether you want to be a part of the solution or another part of the problem.

Gentlemen, Ladies, your spouse is human. Sometimes, they will exhibit non-positive behaviors when dealing with things that make them feel sad, afraid, disappointed, hurt, or angry. And sometimes these feelings are in response to something you said or did ... but it doesn't mean they're being childish, dumb, or their faith's not working. It means God blessed you to marry a human of Earth and not some alien space robot.

In a different vein, sometimes your husband or wife will share personal thoughts or dreams with you that you might think are weird, unrealistic, or just plain crazy. Choose your words carefully. Your spouse needs to feel completely unashamed when they are emotionally exposing themselves to you. It is important to God that your marriage be a place of utmost safety for both of you, spirit, soul, and body. One could say that as a loving member of your marriage relationship, one of your jobs is to help create and maintain a shame-free environment that is safe enough for your spouse to get totally naked in.

Overall, this simple verse, with its few words, is packed full of wisdom. As unassuming as it may seem, its truths will challenge you right to your core. Hopefully, you can see that God is referring to a lot more than a simple lack of clothing. He is referring to a way of being.

Now, please allow me to acknowledge something. Admittedly, some people live very fulfilling lives without ever getting married. Kudos to them because that's amazing in and of itself. I speak of marriage the way I do because it is no accident that the vast majority of people do get married and have families. To the extent that it is broadly considered the normal thing to do.

You see, the programming God put in us before sin and cursing entered the picture is who we are. It's how we are made to function. Now, several thousand years later, the blood of Jesus still provides us the freedom we need to be who He originally designed us to be and function the way He originally made us to function.

This is true of both the man and the woman as individuals, and also of the marriage.

It is an amazing work by Jesus' blood, but sometimes very difficult for us to walk out. You see, man and woman may have the same basic programming as each other, but they are functionally very different. It's the same kind of difference as if one were a dog and the other a cat. They're both mammals, but almost completely opposite of each other. I mean, the closest thing a dog has to purring is a growl... which means something very different.

As men and women, we handle the blessing in our lives differently. We approach making babies and giving life in very different ways. And we naturally walk in authority in different ways as well.

This can't help but make a person wonder how on earth we can work hand in hand to make God's will happen. How are we supposed to be able to do what He wants us to do ... as one flesh?

Well, like all of God's creation, He had a plan. Passion is a big part of that plan, along with Holy Spirit in us and the fruits of the Spirit. He also provided us with some common ground through the same basic programming in each of us. When we do things the way God designed for us to do them, the impossible becomes possible.

SIDE NOTE: This idea of men and women sharing the same base programming is nothing more than saying we both function by the same human nature. The first place I see it in scripture is in Genesis 2:18... "And the Lord said, It is not good that man should be alone; I will make him a helper comparable to him."

When God said this, man was just as much female as he was male. Since they both came from the same original person, it is safe to assume that God was saying it is not good for either of them to be alone. This means a woman needs her man as much as a man needs his woman. Though it may not appear to be remotely the same in how it manifests from each of us, it is still a strong common thread integrated through both of our programming. It's just one example of how men and women can function with the same basic nature even though it looks very different.

Now then, let's continue the discussion of purpose. Staying there in Genesis 2, I've often thought the next few verses to be rather interesting and even comical. They tell the story of how God makes all the animals, birds, and such, and then parades them in front of Adam looking to see which one will be that helper comparable to him. Through the process of it, Adam names all the creatures. Here's a glimpse at how my brain plays out what may have happened.

God: *"So, ah, Adam. What do you think about this one? It has four legs and these super cool horns on its head."*

Adam: *"I don't know. Those horns are really cool, but it's kinda big! Can it talk?"*

God: *"Hmmmm. You're right. Let me see here. There. This one's a bit smaller, only has two legs, but it can talk if you teach it!"*

Adam: *"Yah, but that's another one of those things with feathers all over. I'm still not quite sure what I think about those ..."*

Maybe your imagination doesn't work the same as mine. I think it's funny imagining the two of them sitting there going through all those creatures like a couple of boys in a sandbox, and then still coming up empty. It makes me wonder how many living things God made before finally accepting that it was just not going to happen. Either way, I'm sure they were having a good time working through it with each other, and they did get a lot of work done.

From that, God has the mother of all ideas. He puts Adam to sleep and then takes a part of him out. With the piece now removed, He pumps the boy full of testosterone, sews him back up, and says, "**BAM!**"

Then, with the piece that was taken out, God forms Eve. With her completed, He fills her full of estrogen, closes her up, and says, *"There you are, Sweetie."* (I told you I would paraphrase.)

Now this is an exciting dynamic. Maleness started by having something that was whole and complete, made to be incomplete. A part of his body and an entire section of his personality were just gone. You could say that suddenly, overnight, he became a real boy. You could also say he was leftovers, but I'll leave that up to you.

Femaleness, if you will, began by being taken out of something, like being born. She was inside, safe and protected, and then suddenly she was outside, uncovered and standing on her own two feet. It's no wonder she was the one made to carry and give birth because of the two of them; she is the one who can relate the most to how that feels.

Then God wakes them both up and makes His little presentation to each other.

As would be natural in such a case, when Adam woke up, I'm sure he was stunned and perhaps a little panicky.

He probably felt a little violated, too. Then, upon seeing Eve standing there, he most likely would have sensed the familiarity with her, standing there looking hotter than ever. He probably glanced down at himself and then back up at her, wondering how all of this got all there... and looking like that.

She, being the part taken out, was probably quite freaked out herself. One minute she is safely tucked away, all warm and protected, right there next to his heart. The next thing she knows, she's standing out here, looking like this with these and that, and wondering where on earth his heart went.

Now I'm only speculating, but I think it's highly possible they ran straight into each other's arms. He's there, reaching out, scrambling to grab what was taken from him and trying desperately to get it back where it belongs. She is nestling as deep into him as she can, trying to get back where she belongs. At this point, fear wasn't a part of their reality, so this kind of response seems reasonable to me.

Oh wait! Did I mention they were naked? Yeah, **that** was a moment!

"Then God saw what He had made, and indeed it was very good..." (Genesis 1:31)

And there it is ... the difference between men and women. Men are entirely motivated to physically reestablish that one flesh that was there before any of his parts were taken out ... back to when he was perfect and complete. Women are entirely motivated to get back to where his heart is, enveloped and secure... in other words, back to where she was perfect and complete. They are alike in that they are both driven to wholeness. Yet they are very different in that they go at it from paradigms that appear to be completely opposite of each other.

In the above image, if Adam and Eve did instinctively run into each other's arms, for the first time ever, they would have felt from top to bottom the warmth and tenderness of another person's flesh pressed up against theirs. In this highly emotional and highly energized moment in time, they would have found and felt each other's bodies in newness and raw purity. I believe it's not beyond reason to think they probably became rather aroused and could have easily ended up having passionate sex with each other right there. Their hearts and bodies would have been drawn toward each other in their desperation to get back where they were before.

Yes. I went there. But please don't get caught up thinking that I am making it up to sell my story. Though it does go great with the overall idea of this book, I would more importantly like to inspire your thinking around those moments in time. Think of this event from a very realistic perspective, a very human point of view. What could be considered a believable reality?

I may not be intrinsically accurate about it, but I don't believe I'm all fantasy either. These two people were very real human beings full of feelings and emotions, just like you and me. This event had to be one of the most traumatic and electrifying experiences a couple could ever go through.

Now, whether they actually ran into each other's arms, and whether they ended up having sex right there isn't the point. The critical realization here is that believing Adam and Eve didn't discover sex until Genesis chapter 4, when the Bible first mentions it, is about as far-fetched as believing human beings evolved out of a patch of sludge. By natural law, it's just not humanly possible.

One major piece of convincing evidence is this. When Eve hit the scene, Father God stopped His pursuit of a proper helper for Adam. For Him to do that, He would have had to have seen something between the two of them that let Him know, this is the one.

Think about it. Here are two brand new human beings, all by themselves, and very much attached to each other because of what they had just been through. Additionally, they are the only ones of their species to be found anywhere. In this, they would most assuredly have been captivated by all those fresh new feelings they are discovering within themselves, feelings of love and desire for that other person. On top of this, they have no concept of right or wrong, and nothing but time. Their attentions are consumed with each other, and they are naked ... NAKED! Do we need to keep going?

I mean, your own wife can't even walk naked from one end of the house to the other without you pinning her against a wall or trying to lure her onto the couch, or something. How can you think it's even possible for these two fresh and newly discovering lovers, in the most prime of all honeymoon scenarios, to not get busy even once between then and the time Holy Spirit picks up their story again in chapter 4?

Here's the deal. God was the one who made sex to be a · thing the moment He changed man from being one whole person into a male person and a female person. He formed their bodies so they could fit back together again. He knew when He split them apart, they would be incomplete unless they had a way to become one again. When sex started happening between the first married couple, it would not have been for the purpose of making babies or for pleasure. Sex at its inception would have been the result of the first male trying to reestablish physical oneness with his missing parts, her. Simultaneously, it would have also been the first female trying to reestablish her position in that place of safety, next to his heart. In other words, it would have been all about restoring that sense of wholeness, about becoming one complete person again. This is how we know **sex is for reestablishing wholeness.**

To simplify, sex was not there when man was formed and brought to life. It began when that man became two separate entities, a male and a female. It provided a way for the two of them to reconnect and feel like one person again. The by-products of such are the pleasure and reproduction we are so familiar with today.

This is a big deal. When we objectively look at this for what it is, we can logically and safely conclude that sex is a highly passionate time when a man and his wife are reuniting into oneness. They are becoming one whole person again... thus defining what intimacy is all about.

It also clarifies, beyond the shadow of any doubt, why we are not supposed to have sex before we are married. The only person you can be restored to wholeness with is the person you have a life-long marriage covenant with. Without that covenant, there is no wholeness to be re-established. Simply stating that God made this kind of pleasure, and the rite of reproduction, only for people who are married doesn't provide enough logical reason for people to decide to restrain themselves, whether they follow God or not. It makes more sense, though, when you understand the true purpose of sex, when you see that those two main focal points of our sexuality are just by-products of a healthy love life and not reasons for it. Pre-marital and extra-marital sex are perverted versions of the real thing. Sex within marriage is the ONLY way to experience its true purpose, and the fullness of what it is supposed to be for human beings.

PRINCIPLE ALERT:
This book, again, is written more specifically for people who are married, but if you are single and reading this, listen to what I'm about to say.

If you have any desire in you to remain pure till you say, **"I do",** then you have some decisions to make.

The vast majority of young people who lose their virginity before they get married (referring to those who wanted to stay pure) didn't lose it because they were horny. They lost it because they were focused way too intently on not having sex.

As weird as that may sound, it's true. You just can't focus on sex and avoid it at the same time, even if that focus is indirect. It's not a very fruitful endeavor.

Do not fret. Staying pure is still very possible. If you want to protect your virtue, then you need to adjust your perspective a little. Instead of focusing on trying to avoid sex, you give your attention to avoiding the things that lead to sex.

I'll help you by giving you a few examples. In it, I will call those things for what they actually are, rather than what society has tried to make them out to be.

The first one is making out (passionate kissing sessions that usually include other physically arousing activities). Making out with each other is foreplay. It's an intentional activity that is pointed toward one ultimate goal: sex. It is what a husband and wife do to help each other prepare emotionally and physically for sexual intercourse.

And don't think there is a difference between short make-out sessions and long make-out sessions. Short ones only lead you into long ones, so the final product ends up being the same. Plain and simple, making out has one primary function for why it exists. It activates passion. If you continue to activate passion with your boyfriend/girlfriend, at some point you will not be able to say no and will end up having sex with them... unless, of course, you're stronger than Jesus.

Secondly, touching each other's bodies in places that are not considered to be public domain is another no-no. It is nothing more than playing house (this means you like to act like you're married even though you're not). If Uncle Jeffery can't touch you there, neither can your boyfriend. Why? It's because it fosters intimate feelings that are only free to be acted on by people who are legitimately married to each other. Again, that kind of physical touching crosses the lines of propriety because it fosters those intimate feelings that lead to ... wait for it ... sex!

The last thing I will mention here is a lot alone. This was Adam and Eve. It's probably the biggest, most important truth to deal with in the pursuit of purity. Spending a lot of time alone with someone of the opposite sex will, yes, will, in nearly every case, cause you to fall in love or sin with that person. It is a fact of life that stems from our human nature. You see, as you continue to spend lots of time alone together, you end up in situations where you get comfortable with that person emotionally and physically. Many times, your bodies end up being in close proximity to each other regularly. You become dangerously relaxed with each other. This familiarity and the resulting closeness create a myriad of situations and emotions that fuel passion. And here we go again. When passion shows up, you find yourself emotionally bonded to that other person, and suddenly you're not a virgin anymore. You couldn't say no, and you don't understand how it could have happened to you.

A lot alone... if you are dating and want to stay pure till you get married, do not spend a lot of time alone with your love interest. Period. It's that simple.

Yes. A couple who are engaged and planning for marriage will have times when they are alone together. But as much as possible, it's best for those times to be alone amidst other people (public settings, family, etc.). I think we would all agree that for some reason, when God is the only one who can see us, we have a tendency to forget He is there.

I apologize if all this sounds a little blunt. The truth is that your life is not a toy. It's not something you play with because it's fun. The spirit of the world will most definitely treat you like it is because it does not care about your values or your future. It only cares about controlling you through convenience and pleasure. The cost to you and anyone else who follows its ways is inconsequential to its evil.

The fact of the matter is this. Sex is for people who have spiritually, emotionally, and legally committed their lives to each other forever. Without this commitment, you are only *"awakening love before its time"* (Song of Solomon repeats this phrase several times). So, choose to trust God. He knows what you legitimately need even more than you do. Do not allow the world to form your thinking into how it does dating. Follow Him. You will be incredibly glad you did.

So then, to summarize, the age-old belief that sex is only for pleasure and reproduction is actually a misrepresentation of the truth, a perversion. God's primary reason for creating sex as a part of the human marriage experience is because He knew His man and His woman would need a way to reconnect, to become physically, emotionally, and spiritually one again, and again, and again. It was all about giving them a way to be and feel complete, the way they were originally created to be.

♥ *Perspective* ♥

Now that we've covered purpose, let's change directions and look at what kind of value we should legitimately be placing on sex and sexuality in our marriages. Just how much of a priority is it anyway?

Before we dive in, please let me restate something. As important as I believe our sexuality is, nothing is more important to our lives than God Himself. He is the one who made us. He is the one who brought us together. He is the one who formed us with a fantastic plan for our lives as we grow together in Him. He is our first and foremost consideration.

In the midst of that, let's not forget how the devil has been stealing our marriages and ruining our love for each other for many years now, right under our noses. The whole time he's been doing it, we, with God by our sides, have been holding one of the mightiest weapons on earth to obliterate his assignments for relational destruction. It is passionate love... not the way the world sees it, mind you, but Biblical, holy, passionate love.

So let me say this loud and clear. Sex is NOT naughty! Sin is naughty. Sin is from the devil. The devil did not create sex. The devil perverted it. Perverted sex is naughty. Perverted sex is sin. God made true sex, and it was Him who instituted it into marriage.

Hopefully, we are all still OK. It really is perfectly alright to talk about such things, even though we may feel a little uncomfortable. Sometimes we get so worked up about sex, its relative body parts, and what they do that we would rather blush and turn away than deal with them for what they are. However, the truth remains the same. God made vaginas and penises just like He made ankles and eyeballs. He made them to perform specialized functions for your life and health, and they are just as natural a part of your body as your kneecaps, elbows, or earlobes are.

In the same light, sexually arousing your spouse is just as natural a function of your married life as going to town together or talking about something important. They happen because they are supposed to happen. They happen by God's design.

SIDE NOTE: Let me acknowledge a quick fact. Your love life is a very private thing between you and your spouse.

Let it be known that when I speak about being willing to talk about sex, I am not referring to casually blabbing out your most tender moments or intimate personal details. Just the idea of that is repulsive. It would destroy one of the most critical elements of a passionate love life; a safe, shame-free environment. No, no, no. What happens in your love life stays in your love life.

I am talking about being willing to deal with sex in enough faith to treat it simply and naturally. I'm talking about dealing with it in a mature and very realistic way with each other. We also need to be willing to use that God-given wisdom to train our young how and why they need to be passionate lovers for their own spouses when they get married.

I've said for years that the real strength of any people group is its ability to reproduce after its own kind. Passionate sexuality is no exception to this rule. We need to pass on this truth through our generations, but in a way that does not compromise the sanctity of our own personal intimacy.

Along with that, let me say this. In these days of preparing for Christ to come, it may seem like our sexuality is a nonessential distraction from the main battlefront of spreading the Gospel to all nations. I mean, why look so intently at it now? We have much more critical Kingdom work to do.

I understand that thought, and, quite honestly, I couldn't agree more. So here is why we must take it seriously right now. With the spiritual warfare all around us waging for control over our souls, we need to be able to stand in times of great challenge. Because of this, we have recently seen a major Spirit-led shift back to living much healthier in our everyday lives, especially in the arena of physical health. Holy Spirit has been leading men and women back to the basics of eating healthier foods and exercising regularly. He is grooming us to be steadfast in spirit and the natural things because we need it now more than ever. These daily attentions are a source of strength and protection for us as we traverse these tumultuous times.

In the same way we are getting healthier physically, it is also time to get healthier relationally ... most particularly in the arena of marriage. The spiritual warfare around us is only going to intensify. We desperately need to get back to the basic elements of a true marriage by God's design, focusing on regularly doing the things that bring health and strength to our relationships. To do that, we absolutely must take seriously the value and function of a God-ordained passionate love life between spouses.

The truth is, whether you can get your head around it or not, the devil wholeheartedly believes that we are exponentially more dangerous to him when we legitimately function as one. This is why it is no coincidence that marriages and churches have the worst reputations for their members getting along with each other.

Look, this is a different time than when our parents and grandparents lived. We, as a people in this modern society, deal with issues very differently than they did. It's not as though they did everything right, but they had a lot more grit and gristle about their commitments. They had enough internal fortitude to stay strong through their own mistakes as well as their spouses'. This is evident by how high a percentage of them have been able to stay married for so long ... for better or worse. However, as I just mentioned, that is not where we are today. Now, because of this change, it's time to get serious. It's time to do or die.

So, with that in mind, let's delve deeper into the perspective of making love. Come, let us reason together. Let's talk about what sex is, and what it is supposed to be.

Right off the bat, I believe we can all agree that sex means something different to women than it does to men. This would be due to the difference in the way we began.

Generally, for women, sex is more about being next to his heart. It's about entering that place where she feels protected and connected. This is why most women prefer to have sex behind locked doors, curtains pulled, under the covers, with the lights off. In comparison, we guys are like, *"Hey baby. I know it's the middle of the afternoon, but there isn't anyone in that rest area. We could pull over real quick, get after it in the back seat, and be out on the road again before anybody else shows up!"*

This is also a reason why it typically takes women quite a bit longer to get **'in the mood'**. She must be able to let go of everything else she is dealing with in order to focus on him. If she doesn't know whether or not she turned the burner on the stove all the way off, or if the baby is sleeping, or if the car keys she will be needing tomorrow got hung back up on the peg, she won't be able to close those files in her brain and thus will not be able to feel that sense of security which releases her to think about loving her husband.

The amount of sex she needs is different as well.

Unlike men, God made her in a way where sex is not the only thing that causes her to feel loved and secure. This means sex will only be one of several things that make it happen for her. Because of this, it only makes sense that she will not feel the personal need for sex nearly as much as he does.

Don't get me wrong. There are times when she needs her man to swoop her up to a private place and remind her of how beautiful stars can be. Those times are just not as frequent for her as they may be for us guys.

To further that thought, I'd like to note that many times when a woman needs some loving, she doesn't necessarily know that sex is what she needs. Of course, for us guys, this is as foreign a concept as you can get. For us, we are like, **"How can you not know?"**

I learned this one day because Holy Spirit decided to take me to school. He was leading me out of my old pleasure and reproduction mindset, so He showed me this different kind of value sex could have, and for me, it was way outside the box. It totally blew my mind.

I came home from work one day, and our house was filled with tension. There was my wife, and her mind was running out of control. Her brain was racing; she couldn't think straight, couldn't make up her mind for anything, and she was feeling pressure from everywhere. This chick was stressed (thankfully not because of me)!

Instinctively, up to this point, when I saw my wife like this, I would try to sneak away and hide until I knew it was safe to come out. Then this day happened. Yes, this one magical day, while I was safely tucked away in my office with some video games and a mini-fridge, I heard Holy Spirit say, *"She needs you bad."* (This had to be Holy Spirit because I would never have been brave enough to even dream of going there on my own.).

So, I answered Him, "Needs me bad? Are you kidding me? How's that even work?"

Holy Spirit: "Yah. She needs you bad."

Me: "Do you mean needs me, like, she really needs me to do something? Or needs me like, she NEEDS me?"

Holy Spirit: "She really needs you to make love to her right now."

Me: "I'm just saying, I'm having a hard time seeing it. I mean You are God, though, and you know her better than I do. I don't want to blow you off or be disobedient or anything, so I'm game to try, I guess ... but if I get killed, it's Your fault!"

So, I bravely left my safe place and went to her, looked her in the eyes, and said, "Come with me, sweetie. Let me help you."

I gently took her by the hand, led her upstairs to our bedroom, and proceeded to make her glad to be a woman. When all the stardust settled and we could hear the birds chirping again, I was amazed at how calm and relaxed she was. Her mind was at rest, her stress was dissipated, and all the pressure was gone. She had peace.

Yah Baby! It made me feel like telling her, *"Oh thou, my fairest and most lovely maiden. Your strong and mighty knight has come and vanquished the foul dragon whose horrible spell had you locked in torment. Be free now, my love, and fear nothing, for I am here!"*

OK, so maybe it wasn't quite that epic, but it sure made me feel that way. Not to mention that experience was quite the eye-opener as well.

First, I learned that even though I couldn't fix all the things that were driving her crazy, I could still help her release the stress that was stuck inside, thus restoring a sound state of mind. This enabled her to handle the challenges she was facing calmly.

Secondly, I learned that orgasms have a far greater purpose for married people than just erotic pleasure. We'll dig deeper into that later in this chapter.

The main point here is this. When it happened, she was just as surprised as I was. She thanked me for helping her get back to reality and said she would never have thought of that herself. Somehow, strangely enough, it was just what she needed at that moment, and she didn't even know it.

Holy Spirit did, though. He was there when she was formed. He took me in my ignorance and led me down that path so I could see a little better. I was amazed at the positive kind of impact passionate sex could have on her psyche. Of course, I listened to Holy Spirit even more after that.

I started paying closer attention to my wife. I became motivated to learn and be sensitive to her, and those times when she needed me to slay the foul dragon. Surprisingly, I actually started recognizing more and growing in my understanding of both her and myself.

Then, of course, I'd get carried away thinking that every single time something was a little off, she just needed me to love her, but we all know that's not true. I'd have to reel it in and get back to reality myself, but at least I was learning. The crazy thing is, when I saw how powerful this was, I became motivated to look beyond the physical enjoyment of sex and genuinely try to connect with her. Without even realizing what was happening, my paradigm shifted to being wholly committed to fulfilling her. By becoming more aware of where she was emotionally, I was able to give a more concerted effort to meet her legitimate need. I got good enough that sometimes I would even scare her a little.

By learning to focus on her fulfillment over my own, sex became just as much a spiritual connection as it was emotional and physical. This is because meeting another person's needs before considering your own is what agape love is all about. It's the kind of love only God can give and ultimately work through us.

Consequently, I ended up spending time and effort trying to become a better lover for her. I found educational resources and started learning her anatomy, how different systems work to evoke different types of responses, both sexual and non-sexual (because there is a lot more of life that gets lived outside the bedroom). Essentially, you could say I was learning her mechanics, both her physical and emotional functionality. I was determined to make our everyday lives and our times of lovemaking something worth it to her, even if she wasn't in the mood.

Let me tell you something. Like anything of value in life, being a proper lover can be a lot of work. Especially when you find out, as I did, that a large portion of the lovemaking she needs from you isn't even sexual! (another thing we will get more into later.) It'll make you ask yourself if it's really worth it.

Most assuredly, I can tell you it is, and the resulting fruit can literally save your marriage. It has ours. Building and keeping a healthy, passionate love life is one of the most powerful tools we have in the natural to keep our marriages healthy and strong ... most especially through the younger to middle-aged years of our lives.

The effort you give to learn your spouse and become that passionate, fulfilling lover for them pays off in dividends that go way beyond something as shallow as erotic pleasure. As I just mentioned, it can even save your marriage.

The best way to explain what I mean by this is to share again a little of our own experience and how Holy Spirit helped walk us through it.

You see, even though my wife and I are Christians and want to please God with all our hearts, there have been times when we got overly exasperated with each other. We'd get to a place where we were at the very end of what we could or were willing to deal with anymore. It's not because we were stupid or didn't love God enough. It's because we are human.

We are clearly not the only ones. It shows in our divorce rate. You see, during those ultra-intense times that most marriages go through, neither our love for God nor for each other has proven to be enough to keep us together... a fact I pray this book helps to change.

During those moments when our commitment to each other is at its weakest, what do we have to lean on? If our love for God isn't enough, what on earth can save our marriages and keep us together? I mean, we're obviously missing something because if we were already doing enough of what we are supposed to be doing, the data would be telling a different story.

There you have my wife and me. We've been to that place where we had had enough. It was over. We were done.

If you have also been to that point, you know what I'm talking about. You think thoughts like, **"Yes, God. I know you hate divorce, but you don't have to live with her! I'm done with this! I'll just leave her now and get forgiveness later!"**.

There have been plenty of other times as well when it wasn't quite so bad that we were ready just to walk away, but because of the hurtful things being said or done, restoration was still the farthest thing from our minds.

Unfortunately, these things happen when we humans do what we humans do. Thank God we don't live in those moments all the time. Lord, how could anybody? But they do happen, and I think even more so when you have strong and intense personalities like what we have in our home. As a result, we needed a catalyst for restoration.

So, God, knowing all of this, provided that very thing. He knew it way back when and had a plan. He inserted a powerful binding agent that was so strong it could overpower the angriest of angry, the maddest of mad, or the most furious of furious. It's like His secret weapon for married people.

When my wife and I would get to that point of no return, God would activate it on us. It was ridiculous and amazing how it would diffuse the dynamite.

Funny enough, it was also like a two-edged sword. On one hand, it was great because of how helpful it was to reestablish peace. But on the other hand, it would make us angry because we wouldn't necessarily be ready to give up being mad yet. We would still be committed to forcing each other to deal with their own stupid, hurtful ideocracy (you know, making them apologize first). But even with that, we were still powerless to resist it.

Here's the deal, and how it would play out with my wife and me. Through our commitment to said intimacy, we have developed this fiery passion for each other that burns inside of us. This passion melts us and infuriates us. It's like fire and ice, a raging calm that engulfs our souls. As firmly committed to each other as it can make us feel, it can also stretch those bands that bind us to the brink of annihilation. It's a power that gets mixed up in whatever we do and pushes the pedal to the metal every chance it gets ... and depending on what's at hand, it can either fill us with immense joy or scare the hell out of us!

So, like a boss, when appropriately activated, this passion will burn strife and discontentment up like flash paper. It'll show up right in our faces and force us to deal with how much we truly love each other. It defiantly rises up in the middle of the tumult, grabs us by the nape of our necks, and shoves us straight into each other. This power doesn't give an ounce of thought to whether we are emotionally prepared for what it's about to do. It simply does what it does and then leaves us to deal with it.

Through all that, it becomes undeniable proof, right in front of our eyes, what God means when He says perfect love looks over a multitude of sins.

Its power is maddening because **we can't say no!** We're powerless to resist.

This passion is a true power. A passionate love for each other is God's secret weapon to destroy any attack and annihilate any dart the enemy might throw at you in his attempts to break you up. That passion will blow through your strife and force you to forgive each other, whether you want to or not. It's mighty through God to the pulling down of strongholds and strife and unforgiveness and hurt and...

My wife used to get so upset with me because, at the peak of her wrath, to whatever degree that was, I could melt her heart because I knew how to touch her. The passion that burned in her heart and my ability to ignite it would render her unable to resist, and it would ultimately tear away at the emotional tension between us.

Don't get me wrong. We would still have to work through the thing or things that were making her mad in the first place, but the fire-breathing dragons were back in their dens. We could handle whatever the issues were without any more strife.

It had me too. Seeing her and/or touching her would melt my insides, even when I was furious. She could inadvertently show a little cleavage or accidentally bump into me, causing our bodies to touch, and it would start stirring in me. My angry self would be screaming "**NO-O-O!**" but the hearth fires were already starting to rage. I knew I was weak to it, so when I was fuming, I'd intentionally not look at her, and try to avoid any form of physical contact... even to the point of sleeping as far apart from her in bed as possible. If we touched, I would be a goner and end up giving in first.

Now, when I think back, it makes me chuckle because more than once, when we were lying in bed, intentionally letting the sun go down on our wrath, Holy Spirit had the nerve to interrupt me right in the middle of my steaming batch of angry stew.

He would be telling me I needed to roll over there and make love to her, and He wouldn't stop pestering me until I responded.

I'd be thinking things like, **"Are you kidding me?! You go do that if you love her so much!"**

Now, don't get upset at me here. You can't tell me you've never vented at God about something yourself, especially when you were mad. I'm just thankful that *"He remembers our frame that we are but dust"* (Psalms 103:14), because if not, I would have been burnt to a crisp a hundred times over and a hundred times again.

Either way, my attitude-laced responses were pretty much a waste of time. I learned many years ago, and I'm sure you all have learned as well, just how fruitless it is to argue with God. So, after rustling around in bed for a while, I'd finally give in.

I'd be like that little boy who says to his mom after being made to sit down, **"I may be sitting down on the outside, but I'm standing up on the inside!"** and out of nothing but sheer obedience, I would do what He said.

The fact is, you may not like the taste of the medicine, but it's still medicine. He knew what we needed, and of course, He'd be right. That fiery passion would take over like an all-consuming fire. It would melt away the pain and dissension well enough for us to clear the air. We would find ourselves being able to talk to each other, hold each other, and be restored to wholeness again ... which, by some strange coincidence, happens to be the very functional purpose of sex in the first place!

Look. I'm sorry. You'll have to forgive us. My wife and I are not that perfect little couple who would randomly break out into happy songs while singing birds and smiling woodland animals would come to help us clean our house, bake tasty treats, and make pretty clothes. Many times, our special brand of **'happy song'** did more to scare the animals away than anything else.

We have a lot more peace in our home now, though. And it's because with agape, the only way you lose is if you quit. In the middle of it all, we learned that even despite ourselves, God wasn't falling off His throne. He knows passion all too well.

As a matter of fact, we were probably rather entertaining to Him. We would be in one of those most intense, most heated moments when we were filling His ears with all the horrible, foolish, stupid, idiotic, infuriating, I hate her/him, I should have married somebody else eruptions of emotional fury. He would just smile and cause a lil somethin-somethin to happen that would spark our passions for each other. Then, while still grinning at us, He'd say, *"See. You love each other. You're OK."*

"AARRGGHH!... but thank you."

I'm pretty convinced we've made Him giggle and laugh a lot over the years. I think more than anything, though, He has thoroughly enjoyed watching His secret weapon enshroud us in love and destroy everything the devil worked so hard to do to split us up. After all, it feels really good to make something and then see it do what you made it to do. Right?

Well, thanks be to God, it's worked. We are still passionately married, and yes, God is most definitely still on His throne.

People, if you take this seriously and do it right, you will experience the closest thing to true agape that humans can experience in this physical realm... and it's not naughty.

Let me add another thing to that as well. If you choose to do like the world does and wait for it to be make-up sex, sooner or later, it's going to be too late. Make-up sex, fake-up schmex ... you should try a little blast-that-evil-marriage-busting-devil-back-to-where-he-came-from sex. Make crazy love to each other for the sheer purpose of telling the devil he can't have your marriage. Now THAT'S worth climbing into bed for!

The point here is that having a passionate love for your spouse can and will save your marriage when all your other guards have fallen. And God's OK with it because that's one of the ways He made us to function.

I am entirely convinced that we Christians should be the most passionate, fire-hot, steamy lovers in the whole world. We should be the ones showing the world what they could have if they do marriage right. We should be those people whom the world knows by our love.

I promise you. If we were, our failure rate would not be nearly as high as it is now. Like I told you in the previous chapter, I've met a lot of people over the years who still loved each other but got divorced anyway because *"It just wasn't working out,"* or *"We just don't see eye-to-eye anymore."* or *"We just can't get along,"* or whatever. Yet at the same time, **I've never met a person who divorced someone they were passionately in love with** ... not even one.

Have you?

OK. Relative to the kind of value we should be placing on sex and sexuality in our marriages, we can deduce that we need to take our love life very seriously. We need to do whatever it takes to not only love our spouses, but stay **'in love'** with them (there is a huge difference ... I love my mother, but I am in no way **'in love'** with her, if you know what I mean.)

Our focus needs to be on the relationship. We need to take our eyes off our fallible spouses and set them on the infallible bonds between us. We need to assess and work towards whatever it takes to ensure that our relationships stay healthy and strong, nurturing and fostering our passionate love for each other.

Our goal is to become so in love that no matter what happens, the devil cannot get a wedge in and divide us. We have a responsibility to feed our passions for each other. Then, if or when something happens, it will be there to keep us, heal us, and strengthen our bond. This infusion of relational strength sets us apart because where most couples might break and fall, we stay strong.

Passion is a key element in God's perfect design for your marriage, and as you will see in the next section, our sexuality plays a significant role in feeding and fostering that passion. To put it in perspective, we need to prioritize it accordingly.

♥ What To Do ♥

OK then. We've established that sex is for restoring wholeness, and passion is a force that will bind us and keep us together. So, let's look at how we might accomplish such a goal.

As I stated earlier, your love life is not some remote, isolated issue, like an extracurricular activity in your marriage. It's not in its own special category, tucked away in a cupboard somewhere, for you to take out whenever you need a little fun and fulfillment. It is a main foundational element, and its effects are ever present, even when no one is saying or doing anything with it.

Unfortunately, because this concept of pleasure and reproduction is so burned into our thinking, way too many people view and handle sex like it's a luxury. In their minds, it's kind of like a lollipop to a child, and they handle it accordingly. You see, luxuries are nice when you have them, but are not necessary for life. In other words, if you can survive without it, you don't need it.

I hope that if you don't already, you will soon see that your love life is not a luxury or an extracurricular activity. Even though it isn't connected to physical survival, it is still very much involved in the health of your marriage relationship. This is because, as different as it may sound, when you get married, your number one priority in life, behind God Himself, becomes nurturing, feeding, and protecting the relationship you have with your spouse. It's the most effective way to ensure it never fails and the first step in learning how to feed and foster your spouse's passionate love for you.

When you focus on what the relationship needs, you will still be handling the things your spouse needs, but it will take you even further. It is a truth that you cannot give your supply to the relationship without also giving your supply to your spouse. However, your focus and motivation will impact how you bring it and why you are doing it. Therefore, I'm going to say it again. If you are married, your number one priority in life, behind God Himself, is nurturing the relationship you have with your spouse. It isn't taking care of your job, your house, your friends, family, or even your very spouse. The focus is your relationship and what it needs to thrive in passion.

Now don't let this confuse you. Believe me. This kind of focus will take your commitment to each other to a whole new level... a whole new level. One reason is that it allows you to look past human imperfections. This is good because the imperfections in the humans you love most, like your spouse, can be the most hurtful. Placing your focus on the relationship first allows you to take your eyes off the imperfect person you married and onto the infallible bond between you. In doing so, you are helping to keep your heart in a place free from blame, offense, and bitterness.

This is a big deal. It may not seem like much when you first look at it, but the impact goes deep and is far-reaching. It's like a hidden key that unlocks a secret door in a video game. When you find it and unlock the door, it opens you up to the rest of your destiny, where you can go on and win the game.

I understand you may be questioning the logic behind what I am saying here. It hit me weird when I first saw it myself, so here is where it comes from. When we work through the Bible, we can see the heart of Father God soaked in and through the whole book from start to finish. It is such an encouragement to our souls and an enlightenment to our spirits when we see how much He loves us and cares for our well-being. But His heart is not only on display to encourage us and help us trust Him. It is also to be an example for us to follow. He left us a pattern to see and emulate that will help lead us to that abundant life Jesus referred to in John 10:10.

It resonated through me when Holy Spirit put two-and-two together to show me that Abba Father is all about covenant, and covenant is a descriptor of a kind of relationship. We all understand that Gentiles were brought into the fold after Jesus opened the door for everyone. Still, the true birth of Christianity happened when Father God set a certain people apart unto Himself. He did it by cutting a covenant with Abram (pre-covenant Abraham), thereby creating a distinct and unique relationship with His chosen people.

From that moment on, the condition of the Jewish nation was directly related to how well they fed and fostered their special relationship, their covenant with God. You see, they couldn't deal directly with God. He was invisible to their eyes and purely holy. But that relationship was the connection point that allowed them to interact with their most holy Father. It allowed them to draw on His strength, love, and support. This covenant relationship became so well known that other nations did not fear the Jews themselves but the God they were connected to.

When Jesus came, He expanded the boundaries of this covenant and refined how it functions. Now, in this New Covenant, both Jews and Gentiles alike are welcome, and it's broken down to every individual. This means your relationship will not be affected by what your neighbors do. It is personal between you and Father. This means the attention you give to feeding and fostering your relationship with God will determine your own condition with Him. The relationship is where you are connected. If you keep that connection strong, love and life will flow freely between you. You will meet His need, and He will meet yours.

Now, similar to your covenant with God, your marriage relationship is meant to be a primary source of strength, love, and support. It will help enable you to accomplish all the essential, tangible things in your life. It is the spiritual, emotional, and physical place where you and your spouse are joined together. It is called your marriage covenant. When God said, *"What God has joined together, let no man put asunder"* (Mark 10:9), in every way He was telling us to do whatever is necessary not to allow your relationship to falter. He is saying more than simply keeping your covenant. He is saying to keep it strong.

Now, please don't get flustered by me saying your relationship is your source. Yes, I do understand that God Himself is our ultimate source for life, love, strength, etc. Everything we need we find in Him. But do not forget, the very first thing God gave man to prepare, equip, and supply him for life on earth was each other. He gave them this very relationship. It was after that when He gave them their tangible supply, along with tangible duties to accomplish.

God intended for your marriage relationship to be a primary avenue for bringing His life, love, strength, etc. into your lives. He intended for us to keep it and nurture it, making it strong, because everything you do in your life is either positively or adversely affected by it. You could rightfully say that for a married man and woman, their relationship is the modern-day equivalent of the Garden of Eden. Everything that happens in their lives flows to it and through it, and is impacted by whatever condition it is in.

The only way we can be sure not to put asunder what God has joined together is to fulfill the charge God gave to Adam and **'keep'** the garden, which implies to keep it healthy. When your relationship is kept right, there is a free flow of God's presence moving seamlessly in and through both of you because when you are together as one, you are complete… even when you're upset with each other.

Now, there may be times when God appears to be sharing and ministering to each of you individually, but that's only what it looks like on the surface. Down into the real heart of it, the same healing He brings to one, He brings to the other ... because when one of us hurts, we both hurt. The same direction He brings to one, He also brings to the other, because how can two walk together, lest they be agreed. The same prophetic word He speaks over one of them, He speaks over both because He doesn't call one, but two, as one.

Do you see this dynamic here? Your relationship is so important that it was the absolute first thing God ever gave us. Prudency requires us to handle it with that same degree of priority. We are responsible for doing whatever is necessary to ensure it is strong… strong enough to stand and stand, therefore, till death do you part. In other words, feed it with power… feed it with love… feed it with passion.

I hope this is making sense to you. Your spouse may be the one you are passionate about, the object of your affections, but your long-term success will be determined by how much you feed and foster your **relationship** with them. Because this is a covenant, the more of yourself you lay down, the greater the passion that stirs between you.

SIDE NOTE: There is a reason why the proper focus is such an essential factor in your marriage. Your relationship with your spouse is unique. It is different from any other relationship in your life because it is the only one that incorporates all four types of love with the same person. It is a long-term, live-in relationship designed to carry you through the rest of your life and has an ultimate goal of you becoming one with the other person. From the time you get married to the time you pass away, every step along the journey is supposed to draw you closer and closer together.

Now, of course, there will be other long-lasting relationships in your life, like family or long-time friends, but the success of those relationships is not measured in how **'one'** you become with each of those people. I've said it before. I love my mother, but I am not **'in love'** with her. It's the same thing for the rest of my family and closest friends. Compared to those others, the fact that marriage is so long-term and is powered by passion changes all the rules for how to keep it strong.

Here is an example. Typical relational physics carries the idea that the best way to make and keep friends is to be nice to people. This is simplified, but for the most part, it's accurate. Alternatively, in marriage, simply being nice doesn't cut it. It is only the tip of the iceberg for what is required to make a marriage last. You can have many successful relationships by simply being nice but marriage requires you to die to yourself. That is a very different level of commitment.

Here is the main idea. You cannot use the same relational framework for your marriage that you use for anyone else, including your family and friends.

Keeping this understanding front-and-center is essential in developing unity and feeding passion. Your spouse may be your best friend but your relationship with them is not like any other friend you have. Handling your marriage relationship properly will help protect you from ignorant mistakes. It will help guide you through unfamiliar territory. It'll cause you to do things you know the relationship requires, even if your spouse isn't asking you to do it. It'll cause you to find pleasure in doing mundane things because you're doing them out of love for your sweetheart. It'll even cause you to become more sensitive to their heart (loving what they love and hating what they hate). You'll understand better, forgive easier, and find yourself gazing into each other's eyes more often, falling in love all over again.

Once you understand the importance of focusing on the relationship, knowing what to do next becomes a priority. So, let's look at a practical way to start.

Before we get going, please let me clarify something. As we work through this, I'll be speaking in general truths. We'll be looking at men and women as they are in most cases. It is essential to remember that exceptions to general truths are different from mainstream reality and can always be found when you are looking for them. However, don't forget that there is a reason they are called **'exceptions'**. There will always be those who are legitimately different, but generally speaking, one man's needs are quite similar to every man's needs. And likewise, the needs of one woman are synonymous with the needs of most women.

Now then, since you are in a relationship between you and your spouse, it would make sense to begin by determining the thing each of you needs most, and build from there. This will identify two primary elements your relationship will need to supply both of you.

In that, men typically have one basic need, and everything else they need branches out underneath that one. Women are the same and usually have one basic need as well, with all their other needs branching out from that one.

This would imply, then, that there are essentially two fundamental needs in each marriage relationship, one from him and one from her. Since all the rest of their needs stem from these main ones, we will focus on the two, (Otherwise, this book would probably end up like space and never stop expanding).

The next thing that needs to be employed is straight from the mother lode, so it packs quite a punch. This is so critical that if you are not willing to apply this one principle to what you do for your spouse, then carefully close this book and give it to somebody else. It won't work for you.

The reason it won't work is because the goal here is to feed and foster the passions in your spouse's heart for you, which can only be accomplished if you are willing to go beyond yourself and touch them where they are, in their world, with what they hold dear. So, even though we've already touched on it a little, let's take a moment to explore this reality and drive it home.

Here it is. When you do things to express your true love and passion for your spouse, **do it in their language.**

Here is what I mean. You girls speak female English. Guys speak male English. The linguistics are essentially the same, but the meanings and applications are very different.

He is more about shutting up and just getting it done. She needs to talk it out. He wants to move on because he'll feel better once it's in the past, and she wants to feel better about it before taking another step. He wants to have crazy passionate sex, and she wants to sit on the couch and talk ... and hold hands ... and talk ... and sip some floral tea ... and talk ... and watch the fire burn in the fireplace ... and talk (just wake me when you're ready for bed). His language is grounded in physical connection. Hers is based on an emotional connection.

And to make it even more fantastic than this polar opposite language distortion, somehow, the things that are of the utmost importance to one are typically a meaningless waste of time to the other. How is that for a crazy dynamic?

Seriously! Does God even know what He's doing? (Of course, we know He does, but sometimes it's hard to understand.)

Nonetheless, it is crucial for you to learn how to love your spouse in the way your spouse relates to love. Aside from fostering passion it's one of the most powerful ways to bridge the gap between husbands and wives.

Now I am not saying you need to change how you function and live your whole life. You are still the person God made you to be. But if your focus is to feed and foster the relationship, then, as it pertains to expressing your love to them in the most effective way, do it in the language that speaks loudest and clearest to them. Of course, you can and should express things your way, but the most significant impact will be felt when you are willing to go beyond yourself and touch them in their world, their way.

Here is an example of what I am talking about: On a wonderful afternoon a few years ago, I lit my wife on fire simply by the way I hung some pictures and wall decorations. I wasn't wearing anything that could be considered sexy (jeans and a T-shirt). I wasn't playing any special mood music. I wasn't even looking at her with 'those eyes' or saying lovey-dovey things to her. All I was doing was hanging stuff on the walls ... something I had done many times before.

The only thing I remember doing differently this particular day was making a very conscious decision (to myself) to do everything she asked, just like she wanted it. I did it when she wanted, how she wanted, and with the spacing and angles she wanted to use. I conducted myself as if I were nothing but mindless muscle and made sure to have a happy, supportive attitude along the way.

Look. I didn't feel like messing with that stuff. I didn't understand why she wanted to do things the way she wanted them done. And I still don't even know why it had to be done right then. What I do know, though, is that it was so worth it! I never knew decorating the walls could make her so... make her so... could turn her on like that!

The thing is, my happy-to-do-this-for-you attitude about helping her bring a greater sense of wholeness to her home spoke directly to her heart. It fulfilled her need in the right kind of way to spark the passion in her. Then she fulfilled my need in just the right way to spark the passion in me, but it started with speaking to her in her language, touching her in her world, her way.

Listen, just like my wife in this example, I appreciate it when she expresses love to me in the way she sees and understands love. But I totally connect with her, it lights me up when she expresses her love for me in my language.

Here's a hypothetical example of something I may or may not have ever done in my life, ever. And I'm sure you can relate.

Let's say you, Mr. Husband, were walking by the kitchen and saw your wife at the sink. You decide, **"I'm going to show her I love her!"** So, out of the goodness of your heart, you sneak up close behind her, slide your hand around her hip and upwards to grasp her breast, and then start kissing her on her neck like you do when you're making love.

Now, do you think she will **'feel'** loved by you?

The truth may hurt a little because in reality, you are most likely going to make her feel violated, which is the exact opposite of what you were trying to accomplish.

Will she appreciate your attempt? Probably yes, and will most likely try not to show you how it affected her. But will it make her feel loved and connected to you? Well, Jesus did walk on water, so anything's possible, but NO! It won't.

You will accomplish making her feel like an object of your desire. And though it is good for her to know that she alone is the one you want, it doesn't identify for her where she is in reference to your heart. Why? Because you didn't express your love for her in her language.

For us guys though, if our sweet little lady snuck up close behind us and slid her hand around our hip and upward to hold our chest and then started kissing us on the neck like that, the whole top of our head would blow open, a rocket would launch itself straight up towards the heavens and then explode in the sky filling the world with fireworks and stardust! And even though we know there is no chance of making love at that very moment, we would still be willing to stop the world just to make it happen. You would seriously rock our world, girls, because that's the kind of thing that totally speaks our language.

Her language originates in that inward connection.

His language originates in an outward physical connection.

They are both equally valid, and each one is incomplete without the other. So, when you want to minister to the actual relational needs of your spouse, there is no better way. You do it in their language.

In other words, you don't do what you do for them the way you like to do it. You do what you do for them the way they like it done. It's what makes your love understandable, attainable, and connectible to your spouse. For them, it's what **"I love you"** looks like in everyday life.

As a matter of fact, Jesus did this very thing when He gave up His Godliness to take on the form of man. He gave Himself to learn our language so He could love us the way we understand it most. Oh, by the way. Like with Jesus, did I mention you're going to need to humble yourself?

The first couple of things on our list of what to do are directed at both men and women. For the next couple of sections, I will break it down to be more gender-specific. I want to go a little more into what makes women tick and what kinds of things men can do to minister to her real needs. Then I'll do the same with the men and some things the women can do to meet their real needs. So here we go.

♥ Girls First ♥

You'll have to bear with me, ladies, because I am a man about to talk about women. I understandably know a lot more about what makes men tick, but I do believe I have a measure of understanding of you as well. It is elementary at best, but still proves to be helpful in explaining things to other men. Therefore, I respectfully try to stick to the basics.

OK then, boys. Prepare yourself. Here comes the secret to your universe. Your girl's number one basic need is **security**. Everything about what she needs from life and love comes back to this one thing.

It isn't too complicated. Plus, you've probably heard it many times before. Nonetheless, based on current data about marriage failure rates, you really need to re-calibrate your brains and rethink it. Something is seriously missing because even though we act like we know it, our ladies are somehow still not getting what they need. If they were, the data would be telling a different story.

This is serious. She needs that same secure feeling she had before being removed from original Adam. Having a sense that everything is where it is supposed to be, and the way it is supposed to be, is the very thing that empowers her to be the wife she is supposed to be.

I'd like you to notice that I incorporated the word **'feeling'** into my explanation. This was very intentional, because though you may be providing and maintaining the things she needs, it isn't enough to just put them in place around her. In her world, the way you do what you do is just as important as what you are actually doing. In other words, it's your deeds and your ways that provide for her the kind of environment that makes her feel secure.

This is where most of us fall short because it already takes a lot of focus and effort to simply provide the things she needs. When we put that much energy into a thing, other issues tend to fall out of our consciousness. But as natural as it may be for us to only focus on the actual provision, it is still equally necessary to present those efforts the right kind of way as well.

"So, you're telling me I have to change the way I like to do and say things to accommodate the way she feels?"

YES! You're getting it! You need to change the way you naturally say and do things to accommodate the way she feels: the way she feels loved. You must stop pridefully holding on to your own precious methods, no matter how comfortable they are. You need to learn **and** adapt yourself so you can work towards meeting her needs in a way that communicates love to her, (I told you focusing on the relationship would take your commitments to a whole new level!).

This is the ultimate goal. Here again, it is not simply meeting the need, but meeting it in a way that makes her feel loved throughout the process. The only way to accomplish this greater purpose is to humble yourself and be willing to change.

"Wait a minute! Isn't that something we are supposed to do to grow up as Christians anyway?"

YES! You're getting it! You are supposed to do this to grow up as Christians anyway!

Think about it. Most of you (hopefully) can agree that God gave you your wife. God is also the one who created marriage and established its proper function. In other words, He knew what the needs of your specific spouse would be. Therefore, He knew where you would need to change and develop when He brought you together. Chances are pretty high that one of the reasons He gave you **'that'** wife was so you would change and grow in those specific areas. This whole idea about humbling yourself and adapting your methods isn't all about her. It's also because that is where God needs you to grow for His greater purposes as well.

What a God! To think He would come up with such a plan. He made the requirements for becoming the right kind of lover for your spouse to also be the exact requirements for becoming the right kind of Christian for Jesus. Brilliant!

It makes a lot of sense, though. Being both a proper Christian and a proper spouse can only happen through agape. Agape love is God's kind of love and is the one and only way for us to become who we are supposed to be in this life.

So, ring the bells and sound the horns. There you have it. Yes, guys, she needs security. She needs you to provide what satisfies her sense of wholeness, and in a way that makes her feel safe... which from this point forward will be referred to as an **'atmosphere'**. We provide the atmosphere she existed in before God put Adam down for his nap.

OK. Now that we have the basic idea down, let me help you by bringing in a little more clarity. In this physical realm, there are a number of things that can help create and provide this sense of security for her. Among them, there is one that rises to the top of almost every woman's list. Strangely enough, this one thing is a main thing for the vast majority of women around the world. It has manifested in women from the beginning of time all the way up to the present day, and beyond. This most popular and timeless element can be encapsulated in one simple word ... **home.** She needs a home.

She needs her house, with her husband, with their furniture, with their dishes, with their decorations, and with their children, with their... etc. She needs it to be saturated with a love-rich environment so she can freely care for and nurture everything in her space. And she needs it all in good working condition, so it doesn't feel like she's falling apart.

Ladies, would you agree?

You see, boys, though security may be the ultimate goal, one of the biggest ways it translates through female English is **home**. In a proper home, there is a sense of safety and love that ministers to everyone in it. Most importantly, it ministers directly to her heart. A home with this environment, this atmosphere, is the foundation for what she needs most.

As a man, you need to stay mindful of this because, as much of a need as this is for her, she can't create it all by herself. She needs you to do it with her and for her. Your willingness and commitment to work with her to attain and establish your own personal space, her home, is one of the most effective ways to show her, in her own language, how much you care.

Now, the process of developing this home will require another of her absolute needs: communication, or, in other words, talking to each other.

We have all heard for years how important this is for a marriage. Effective communication is the key to unity. It's the key to working together, the key to keeping things transparent. It's the key to honesty and the key to resolving conflicts. As a matter of fact, if I asked a hundred different people what activity is the most important for a married couple to engage in, probably eighty to ninety of them would say **'communicate.'** We have heard it backwards and forwards and crosswise and sideways and upside down and inside out and any way you look at it, and yet we guys still don't want to talk about it.

This is one of those areas that we all seem to know because of how much we hear about it, but in truth, we really don't know because of how lackadaisically we walk it out. Essentially, how it typically pans out is we'll be willing to talk about stuff we know is vital to her, but only when we feel like it.

This can be tough because, although we typically have all kinds of reasons why we don't feel like engaging in conversation, it usually comes down to one thing. It is because of how we are wired. Just sitting and talking goes directly opposite of how we naturally deal with stuff. So, when we say we don't feel like it, we truly, from the depths of our beings, do not feel like it. Having to start talking and sharing from our hearts goes against our grain so much that it makes us uncomfortable. It's a pain to try and figure out what words we can say that express what we think without hurting our girl's feelings. For us guys, our words and our emotions are two like poles on a magnet. They naturally repel each other. And don't worry. We are more than happy to go with that flow, keeping them as far from each other as possible.

This is such a big deal for us that if you gave a man the choice of being dragged outside, tied up to a post, and given a good beating or sitting down to just talk and share his feelings about a thing, most men would take the beating. It would take less time, and upon completion, it would be over and done with, allowing us to move on with the rest of our day. Yes. According to our psyche, the beatings have a much better survival rate.

The problem with this is Agape. Agape is essential for your marriage to thrive, and it requires you to prioritize the needs and feelings of your spouse above your own. In marriage, it's what sacrificial giving is all about. In other words, one significant way we guys lay our lives down for our bride, like Jesus did for His, is to be willing to go beyond our natural, most comfortable way of doing things so we can minister to her need right where she is, in her world, in her language.

It comes down to this. Your relationship needs you to talk and share with your wife. So, no matter how much this goes against your grain or how bad you are at it when you get married, you still need to grow and develop your ability to communicate your heart and feelings with your wife on a regular basis.

Listen guys. This is not an option for her. In the very same way you give, receive, and process your emotions through physical activities, she gives, receives, and processes her emotions through spoken words. Refer to the magnet example again. As much as your words and feelings are **'like'** poles that repel each other, her words and feelings are **'opposite'** poles that are drawn toward each other. They will forever be indelibly connected. In other words, it is equally as difficult for her to refrain from meaningful conversation as it is for you to engage in it.

After years of living with myself, I've learned this gets really difficult in those areas I have no interest in. It isn't so horrible having to talk about things I like, or even things I'm indifferent about. But don't bother me with things I don't like. I resist them. They do not deserve my attention or effort, so I shouldn't be forced to waste my time on them.

Maybe you're not like that, but either way, remember what I mentioned earlier. For some reason, it seems like whatever is most important or meaningful to one is usually a worthless waste of time to the other. Those very things that disinterest you the most are probably near and dear to the heart of your spouse. Proceed with care because treating things that you know are very important to someone's heart with disgust or disinterest will make them feel like you are disgusted with or disinterested in them.

There it is. As well established as it has already been, another vital way to minister to your wife's greatest need is by being available to listen to her and share from your heart. Engage in meaningful conversation.

Let me encourage you guys by letting you know this kind of communication is probably not as difficult as you think. It doesn't always have to be some deep emotional experience that sucks you into a vortex of psychological relativity, ending up feeling more like a therapy session. You can have a meaningful conversation about silly things, like a fly that got its leg stuck in the screen while you were gone. You just have to be willing to engage with her and re-experience her discovery through her telling of the story. Demonstrating genuine interest in her and what she has to say is the element that makes it meaningful.

Now we've addressed the importance of providing a home, which is as much about atmosphere as it is about the building. We've also acknowledged the elephant in the room by reiterating the importance of meaningful communication. The next thing I'd like to bring to your attention is the need to treat her as a weaker vessel. This idea is borrowed from 1 Peter 3:7, and it holds enormous potential. If this scripture is new to you, don't get upset. The Bible does not say women are weaker than men. God doesn't get caught up in such nonsensical discussions (an example we all should follow). It tells husbands to dwell with their wives with understanding and then give her honor as if she were a weaker vessel.

Let me share some practical knowledge about this verse. To treat your wife as if she is a weaker vessel without hurting her feelings, you will need to acknowledge and establish with her that you do not believe she is a weaker vessel. You must create a culture that speaks to her and treats her as your equal. She is your partner for life. She needs to feel like her input and understanding, her skills and perspective, are as valuable and necessary as yours are. This is lived out in the way you treat her... with understanding, giving her honor.

Here is a fair warning, though. Another thing the Bible tells us is *"... out of the abundance of the heart the mouth speaks."* (Matthew 12:34). This means that no matter how you try to sugar coat or fake it, if you genuinely believe she is weaker, your heart will give you away. Your overall communication will rat you out, and she will know. For you to treat her as if she is a weaker vessel while fully understanding she is not, you need to get your own mind and heart right first. You will need to *"bring every thought into captivity to the obedience of Christ"* and *"be transformed by the renewing of your mind"* (2 Corinthians 10:5 and Romans 12:2, paraphrase).

On the flip side, some women view this stronger-to-weaker dynamic as some standard of equality. This is a mistake. Now I'm not here to delineate about equality, so if you intend to start that argument, I will sorely disappoint you. I want you to know; this verse is not even remotely making reference to whether men and women are equal.

This verse was inspired by God but written by a man... to other men. In Male-English, this concept of her being a weaker vessel resonates deeply within us men, highlighting how we need to handle our wives by focusing on two elements that are monumental in a man's psyche: honor and respect. Peter is ensuring that all the men understand the importance of treating their wives with honor and respect.

We all know the reality of it. There are areas of life where men tend to be stronger than women. We also know there are areas of life where women are stronger than men. We were made to complement each other. Where one is weak, the other is strong, and vice versa. We can compensate for our weaknesses by working together as one.

Even further, let me debunk the equality idea even more by playing the devil's advocate. Let's pretend for the sake of this example that women are a weaker vessel than men. So think of it like this, it's like we are hosting a big three-legged race, and these married folk are the contestants. After all, being married means two people functioning as one, much like the contestants in a three-legged race. So, we have all these couples, each person with one leg tied to the other person's leg.

Now, think hard about this. With full knowledge that she is the weaker person of the two, which person on the team is the most important? Does his greater strength make him more crucial to the team's overall success?

As Paul would say, **"God forbid!"** A strong man carrying a weaker woman in a three-legged race (otherwise known as marriage) will still lose to a man and woman working in unity with each other. You will always get more done more quickly when you each humbly treat each other with honor and respect, learning to work together for a common goal. This means even if women are legitimately weaker than men, the level of their individual strength is still irrelevant. They are both equally necessary to the success of their union.

OK. I am done playing the devil's advocate now. We are going back to normal because I want to stress this once again to you husbands. Respect her intelligence. Honor her presence. Make her feel like, next to God, her opinions are the most valuable to you. And in the middle of that, treat her like she is a precious and delicate treasure.

So, then, everyone should be aware that overall health is tied to a complete, healthy diet. We need to eat food from all the food groups because of the unique nutritional value each group brings. Additionally, they work with and through the nutritional values provided by the other groups. They are all necessary to facilitate your overall health. Guys, the things I've written about your wives so far are like the meat, the muscle-building protein to her relational diet. As enriching as these things may be, she still needs her fruits and vegetables to stay healthy. These are the things we will start adding next.

To make it a little more streamlined, I have listed several things to consider in helping to establish the right kind of atmosphere for your wife. These are things that would speak 'love' to her in her language. Some are physical, while others involve how you approach life (your lifestyle has a significant impact on the kind of atmosphere you create). Keep in mind that this is all about fostering your wife's passion, so she may not relate to everything on this list. You will need to talk to her to find out what speaks to her the loudest in terms of love. Additionally, this list is intended to help guide you in the right direction. It is not comprehensive, so feel free to add to or take away from it according to your wife's input.

I will not include getting her a home, engaging in meaningful conversations, or treating her as a weaker vessel. These are at the top of this list, but not included, because we have already discussed them. So here we go:

- ➢ Have a plan, with goals for your life.
- ➢ Do well on your job.
- ➢ Make sure your financial obligations are taken care of… on time.

- Be honest and truthful with her, especially with how you feel about things.
- Speak respectfully, use words and tones that make you sound like you care.
- Be a man of conviction.
- Pray with her and for her (lead her in the Word and prayer)
- Have Self-Control ... be led by your spirit, not your emotions.
- Holler little, listen much.
- Value what she says.
- Be humble ... willing to be wrong.
- Be strong, be gentle.
- Be sensitive, considerate.
- Demonstrate thankfulness and appreciation for her and what she does.
- Defend her.
- Fix broken things before she asks, or at the very least, when she asks.
- Randomly do a task for her that she would typically do herself.
- Notice her, (Is she happy or sad, did her hair differently, wearing something new?). Show interest in her world.
- Pay attention to her likes and dislikes... respond accordingly.

- Be romantic – work to get her to fall in love with you all over again.
- Bless her with random acts of 'love you'.
- Date her… regularly and take her out.
- Learn how to be her lover… how to make her glad to be a woman.
- Shower her with non-threatening affections
- Dance with her (clear space in the room, set the lights, play the right music and dance the night away).
- Regularly express how much you love her and how she is the only one you want to grow old with.
- Hold her ... hold her hand, hold her close, hold her by being there for her, etc.
- Enter her gates with praise and her courts with thanksgiving.
- Smile and be cheerful.

Notice how many of these are sexual?

I'm quite sure you ladies could easily comprise a list that would blow mine out of the water. The idea, as stated above, is to give you an idea of the kinds of things you can do or be to help establish a secure atmosphere in your home. The real gold will come straight from your wife, though. Talk to her, learn from her. Then keep that communication going so you can stay current with her through changing times and seasons.

SIDE NOTE: If you are reading this as a single man still preparing for a bride, pay very close attention. If you have the wherewithal to focus your attention on developing yourself in these areas, you will start becoming the man your future bride needs you to be right now. Then, when the time is right for you to find your girl, you will not have to look very far. You will most likely have several who are already close to you in your life, all hoping to be the one you choose. Why? Because you will be that rare gem who is already the kind of man she needs and is looking for.

So then, let's take this discussion a little farther from shore. From the above list, one of those items was about non-threatening affection. I wanted to make a special note of this because the whole concept of it will wreck your brain. The translation is that she needs you to give her affection that is not driven by sex.

Further translation, she needs to know and feel that you love her, '**the person**', not just her, '**the sexy collection of your favorite body parts**'.

I understand this doesn't make a lot of sense to you guys because, hey, how is that even possible?! For us, love, sex, and physical affection are all part of the same thing. To try to come up with a way to have one without the other would require systemic reprogramming. A simple software update would not be good enough. We would seriously need to completely recalibrate our brains and learn how to do things in a totally different way from the... Oh wait. That is the whole point here, isn't it?

This is a very real deal for her. She needs you to hold her hand, kiss her forehead, massage her neck, hug her, hold her, etc., but in a way that doesn't make her feel like you're setting her up to get a little. She needs to feel that you love her just as much sexlessly as you do sexually. It's a big part of how you cherish her and demonstrate her value to you.

I call this learning the art of sexless love making. Yes. Make love to her without taking her to bed, which involves affection and a whole lot more.

This art starts with being willing to change what motivates you. Instead of fixing or doing things because they need to be fixed or done, intentionally do them out of a choice to express love to her. Let everything you do become an expression of your love.

This can be tough because even if you are just taking out the trash, if you are doing it as an expression of your love for her, you'll do it when she wants and the way she likes it done. Why? Because your purpose is not only to get the stinky trash out of the house. It is to make her feel loved by how you get the stinky trash out of the house.

Now you may be thinking, **"Does that mean I have to do every single thing she asks me, and when she asks me to do it?"**

The answer is no, because sometimes circumstances don't allow you to. However, the way you handle those times will make all the difference in the world for whether she still feels your love. The willingness of your heart says everything to her.

Again, you are making a conscious choice to fix and do things about your home and life as an expression of your love for her. Holding true to this motivation keeps your purpose front and center in your mind, where it needs to be. It not only guides what you do, but also how you do it. It assures her that you are committed to her on every level, that you value her, and that she is connected to your heart. It's a significant way to feed and foster her love for you... sexless lovemaking.

I understand the terminology may sound a little weird, but if you think about it, making love is simply creating love, or doing something that makes another person feel loved by you. Sex has been the one main activity attached to this concept for obvious reasons, but sex is not the only way to make someone feel loved by you, especially with ladies. Therefore, it behooves us husbands to look beyond sex in our endeavors to make love to our wives.

Here again, it is essential to find out what things speak the loudest to her. Those are the things she needs from you. By learning them and choosing to do them, you are, by definition, doing something that makes her feel loved by you... making love.

This concept is not new. God is the one who brought it up in the first place. You can see it right there in Colossians 3:23: *"And whatever you do, do it heartily as to the Lord..."*

In the context of marriage, this verse would read, *"And whatever you do, do it lovingly as to your wife ..."*

It's the same thing! Once again, spiritual growth and marital growth look exactly alike.

Take up the challenge to make her feel more loved outside the bedroom than she does in it. I know this wrecks your brains because having a pretty lady to physically enjoy is, at some fundamental level, the main reason you married her in the first place. But, you must remember, it is an honor to God when you give yourself to loving your wife selflessly in this way. He calls it living with her according to wisdom. It is agape.

Don't worry. Sex still does have its part in making her feel connected to you. However, as we've already discussed, it's just one thing on a list of things that all contribute to the same goal. Unfortunately for us guys, it's usually farther down her list in terms of importance. It's there, and it is important. It's just not the most important.

If you haven't picked up on it yet, this is another one of those areas where we guys need to humble ourselves before the mighty hand of God and be willing to change our methods. It's one of the ways we lay our life down for our bride, the way Jesus did for His.

Now, then, one other item from the list above that warrants a closer look is **'random acts of love you'**. These are very much a part of sexless love making. These types of things carry significant weight. Surprise her with some flowers, a card, or a gift. Leave a special little chocolate with her coffee, send her a thank you note, or sneak home before she gets there and make her a nice dinner.

All these sweet little **"I'm thinking of you"** gestures happen to be a significant part of what makes her feel connected to your heart. As a matter of fact, because these types of actions are so meaningful, your little effort may cause all the planets to line up making it a very happy day for you, if you know what I mean. There is no guarantee of such a thing, so don't jump to conclusions. However, you're a fool not to participate. Quite simply, she's worth it no matter what, and this is a major way for you to stir up those passions within her.

This is such a significant expression that books have been published solely for the purpose of giving men ideas about random things they can do for their wives. Take the hint and run with it. As you do, remember that doing these things here and there is very good, but the real treasure presents itself when you make it a part of your lifestyle.

As we move forward, please let me clarify once again that it is OK to be sexual with her. The key is in the balance. Just because she needs sexless love making from you doesn't negate the fact that she does still need you to romance her and sweep her off her feet. Sex is still on the list.

To help you guys with some perspective, let me offer you a little more of a mechanical approach. Let's say you've talked it out and your wife's list of things that make her feel loved and secure has five main items on it. Assuming sex is one of those items, then her need for sexuality from you is at a rate of 1 in 5. This is the mathematical equivalent of 20%. This means that to accurately meet her needs, 80% of the love you express to your wife should be in the realm of sexless love making.

Now, there may be other factors involved, such as the equivalency of the portions and the intensity of the need, but at the very least, this is a good place to start. Then all you need to do is apply this equation and make it manifest in your everyday life. No problem! Right?

It is all about balance. This is an area where we seriously need Holy Spirit to help us. Trust me, boys. A time is coming when you will be thankful you learned how to feed her needs this way.

Above all, it comes down to this. She needs to know that you want her back where she belongs, tucked safely up next to your heart. She needs to feel connected and valued by you, like she is a part of you. We husbands are responsible for providing that for her ... a home with a safe, love-filled atmosphere that makes her feel like she is where she belongs.

Why? Because this is how we husbands feed and foster passion in our wives' hearts. This is how we protect and strengthen our relationship with her. This is how we let no man put asunder what God has joined together ...

♥ Then The Boys ♥

OK Girls. The thing we guys need more than anything else in life, even more than air and food, is security. That's right. I said security. I did not say sex. Though sex is a decent part of it, our core need goes deeper than that. We draw confidence from knowing our missing part is with us. This means being united with us, supportive of us, believing in us, and desiring to be one with us. This, of course, manifests through physical affirmations, which is where the idea of men needing sex comes from. The more profound truth is that we need physical oneness because physical oneness is what love and support look like in the language we speak. In other words, when we receive regular doses of this physicality, it creates an environment rich in physical connection, emotional security, and spiritual oneness in us.

Now I know mankind has, for a very long time, stuck mainly to the simple conclusion that men need sex. This is wholly and entirely an incomplete conception of the truth. Now I am not refuting the fact that men need sexual fulfillment. Still, I wholeheartedly disagree with the idea that you can minister directly to the need of his heart by simply satisfying his flesh. As a man, I have experienced a lot of frustration because I knew our connection to sexual activities went much deeper than just bodily urges. I couldn't figure out what that connection was, though, or how to say it. Until I was able to construct a solid defending argument, I had to do what every other man has had to do and simply accept it for what everyone says it is.

Beyond that, men themselves have propagated this simplified idea as much as anybody else has. Even though we might know there is more to the story, we tend to avoid deep emotional interactions. If we can get away with generalizing and simplifying our complex emotional structure, we will do it nearly every time. It is so much easier to stick with the status quo here and just say we need sex. I mean, it isn't wrong. Otherwise, we would have to go digging down deep into ourselves and deal with the why, the how, and the what for. Then we would have to figure out a way to explain it. In our minds, it's just better to keep it simple.

Unfortunately, with the lack of any perceived emotional or spiritual connection, coupled with the prevailing mentality that sex is only for pleasure and reproduction, this generalized idea about men opens the door for most people to think men are just addicted to sexual pleasure. It's as if God made men with a predestined addiction to satisfying his flesh. Which implies his need for sex is pretty much the same as an alcoholic's need for booze. The addicted may think it's highly necessary in their life, a need, but those who know better can see it's just the addiction talking. They could live without it if they would just *"be strong in the Lord and the power of His might."* (Ephesians 6:10).

This thought process also implies that when a man gets married, to ensure it will last, the first thing he needs is deliverance.

Well, without greater definition or more specific parameters, it's very natural for our minds to subconsciously default to the next available explanation that seems to make sense. As natural as this is, it is a danger, especially for you girls. The way you naturally function will cause you to think and feel as though this kind of obsession with physicality is very shallow. It's like juvenile puppy-love type stuff with no actual depth. The reality is, most men who have been married for any length of time are not being driven to be physical by an addiction to, or need for, sexual pleasure (which would be juvenile puppy-love type stuff). He is driven by a deep-seated drive for wholeness, and the sense that their connection is sure and steadfast... secure. But if you choose to stick to generality, though, this truth will rarely be the explanation your subconscious latches on to. In that case, let the misunderstandings begin...

Look. Men's flesh-level obsession with physical activities cannot be denied. Doctors will even tell you that, on average, sexually active men will typically need some form of sexual release every three days or so. There is undoubtedly a part of his drive that stems from his body, but that physical element is only part of the picture. The emotional and spiritual connection produced becomes a more powerful magnet that keeps drawing him back for more.

Here it is in a nutshell. For us men, our physicality and the need for it are directly connected to how we express emotions. In the same way women express and receive emotions through their words, men express them through physical action. A typical husband who constantly touches his wife is not being a perverted juvenile with no self-control. He is expressing his emotions through the language of men. He is telling her how much he loves her and desires to feel connected with her. Now he would do himself well to read the previous section, because if that is what he is trying to do, he will not effectively convey his true heart for her unless he flows through her parameters. Too much of that sort of thing doesn't translate well into her language. But the truth remains. His physicality is much more about his need to feel connected and secure than it is a drive to satisfy a physical desire. Because of this, the best way for a wife to minister to his true need is through physical affirmation. Even though her words are essential, the focal point of her communication needs to be physical.

In fact, our internal wiring is so interconnected with her physical affections that when it goes missing, we fall apart emotionally. We can lose confidence, forget our purpose, become incredibly insecure, quite irritable, and struggle to have hope for a happy life. And yes. This sounds pathetic, but most of us have come to accept this about ourselves.

It also messes with the concept of the five love languages because for us guys, physical touch is the baseline for almost all of our communication. And then there are those who really have it bad. Not only is their male English based on being physical, but their primary love language is also physical touch. I am one of those, and sometimes I drive my poor wife absolutely crazy. You all pray for her.

Either way, we are very outward, eyesight, and touch-oriented people. We can get aroused by just looking at our lady (and she doesn't even need to be naked). Then, when we see the thing we like, we are driven to touch and play with it.

As I hinted earlier, this outward-in orientation puts you girls in an awkward position because of how opposite you are in the way you function. To you, this preoccupation with all that physical stuff is again shallow, juvenile, or even insulting. It isn't natural for you to think those physical encounters are the emotional connections of your husband's heart. But they are, even if you have to convince yourself of it. They are how love and emotions work for him.

So then, as a general truth we all understand the need for respect, verbal encouragement and support from one another. It is a vital part of developing positive communication and sharing support with your spouse. But more specifically, these are not the most effective ways to make your husband feel loved by you. Are they important? Yes. But when you are giving this kind of support, you are speaking with your mouth. When you are saying **"I love you"** to your husband in the language he knows best, **'you let your body do the talking'**.

He needs you to cover him with your Femininity. Enshroud him with your touch. Work to get him so accustomed to your body being there with him that he feels like you, the rib, were never taken out in the first place.

Now you may be thinking, "With all these references to physicality, what is he actually talking about?"

Not to worry, girls. Like with the guys, I have comprised a list of several things to help give you an idea of how this physical-based emotional security can be accomplished. Whatever you do though, please do not reduce these things down to a mere desire for sexual pleasure. That conclusion will lead you farther from the truth. This list isn't for helping your husband live out his wildest fantasies through you. It is very serious, and all about helping you work with the way he was made so you can create that environment of love and wholeness in him. Please read with an open mind.

Here we go ...

➤ Go with him to places he likes.
➤ Sneak up behind him and tickle his back with your breasts.
➤ Randomly plant kisses on him, not just his lips.
➤ Go to him and gently press yourself up into him, enough to make him think about what's happening.
➤ Wait till he's just about to walk out the door to go somewhere, flash him a breast and say, **"She's thinking about you."**
➤ Sit on his lap.

➢ Sit next to him and nestle in.

➢ Help him work on something.

➢ Hide a cutsie pair of your panties in a place you know only he will find them.

➢ Make him some breakfast, wearing not but a pair of panties and one of his button-up shirts.

➢ Pull him aside and tell him you need him to make love to you immediately.

➢ Pull him aside and make love to him immediately.

➢ Give him a coupon good for one 15-minute massage session ... if you're brave enough, make it topless.

➢ As he's sitting, go to him and gently nestle his head into your chest, assuring him of how much you appreciate him.

➢ Hold him when you are next to him.

➢ Have him lie his head on your lap and gently stroke his hair (or scalp if…).

➢ Go for a walk with him.

➢ Get some new moisturizer and ask him to help you rub it all over your body.

➢ Take a shower with him... get all lathered up and then wash his body with yours.

➢ If you're going to be home alone for the evening, go braless and let him know you're doing it just for him.

➢ When you're out in public, grab and hold his hand before he can grab yours.

- ➢ When you're out in public, take his arm and let him lead you.
- ➢ Greet him with a hug and kiss when he gets home.
- ➢ Keep him company while he is working on a project.
- ➢ Take his hand and place it on a part of your body he likes and tell him, **"You looked like you needed something."**
- ➢ Treat him like he is the stronger vessel… like you are depending on him to protect you and provide for you.
- ➢ Enter his gates with praise and his courts with thanksgiving.
- ➢ Smile and be cheerful.

So, ladies … ladies? OK girls. Take your left hand and start raising it so that your fingers rest gently underneath your chin. Good. Now press upwards slowly until you feel your lips touching again. Awesome! Good job!

This list is far from comprehensive. And I'm sure you noticed there are several entries incorporating your breasts. There is a reason for this, but we'll get more into that in chapter 3. For now, please note that all these things are not absolute requirements. I'd like to share some ideas of the kinds of things that will resonate with his heart. The concept is that anything you can do to connect your husband to your femininity, your feminine body, will draw him into connecting with your heart. And as you can see, it doesn't always mean you have to get naked. The real gold will come straight from your husband. Be brave enough to ask him what kinds of things he likes and take what he tells you into consideration.

Again, let me encourage you. Do not go reading too much into this list, thinking I'm trying to create some fantasy world here. I am being very sincere, so think of it like this. God gave you this body and then wired your husband to connect to your heart through your body. So, use it! Do with it what God would have had in mind when He installed the software (or if you will, hardware), that makes your hubby go crazy over it.

There is nothing else on earth that will feed and foster his passion for you like expressing your love for him physically. In the language of his heart, it is the very thing that takes your love from being logos to rhema, from being a logical understanding to a living revelation.

I understand that this likely feels very awkward for most of you girls because you are all about deep calling unto deep, uniting hearts through that inward connection. Compared to that, this shallow level physical stuff seems like playing around, like it could never amount to anything real. But let's go through it again. God made us guys to be outward-in. Before we get into the depths of our emotions to make that inward connection, we must first go through the surface level, outer flesh. When you speak love to us through outward physical affirmation, it opens our hearts. It makes us want to share inner things with you. I don't know how, but it softens our tough outer shell and welcomes all the mushy emotional stuff we usually try to avoid.

To put it simply, our drive and desire for your physical body is the demonstration of our need to be connected to your heart. Your physical love is our emotional support. It's the thing that assures us that your heart is committed to ours. It is our security.

It's the craziest thing, too. When my wife physically demonstrates her love for me, it makes me feel like I can conquer the world. It makes me want to bite the heads off dragons, build an empire with their bones, and then sit with her and brush her hair while telling her all about my experiences, and how they made me feel.

Destroy the dragons! Connect with the princess! Hoo-rah!

So then, this is probably the main area where you girls need to be willing to humble yourselves enough to recalibrate your brains. Letting your body do the talking isn't a juvenile game of patty-cake. It isn't about trying to get attention or anything immature. It is purely focused on feeding and fostering his passion for you in his own world, his way.

I want to point out that not all of these things would need to be done all day, every day. Though certain affections should happen every day, such as hugs and kisses, spoken love, and meaningful conversation. The rest would be things you sprinkle in amongst those regular activities. Go ahead and maintain your mystery, but be creative and have fun with these things, too. You will become skilled at randomly blowing his mind, instantaneously interrupting his brain. You will send him flying so high he'll need to call you to help him find his way home.

And then you can take it a step further, stepping into the meaning of a true helpmeet by using it to minister to him. Like you, there will be times when he needs more love and tenderness than what is typical, because of what he is dealing with in life. If you pay attention, you will be able to sense when something is off. You can tell when he's been dealing with tougher, more stressful things, and you'll want to be there for him. In those times, don't start by asking him a bunch of questions about why, what, and who, trying to get him to talk about it. And for sure, don't jump down his throat for being testy or unhappy. Just gently let your body talk to him a little bit. Let the anointing that only you can bring minister to him through the language of your touch. Let your tenderness be like the showers in Psalms 65:9-10 and soften the hardened furrows that have developed on his heart.

It'll reach him because it's the language of his heart. It'll remind him of some things before he gets around to opening his mouth, which is a good thing. You could be diffusing a potentially intense conversation before it even begins.

There will also be times when he needs you to take him to bed and reboot his brain. Giving him some passionate love can flush away a lot of the negative energy that may have built up inside of him, thus helping him deal with his situations in a much better frame of mind. Also, it'll help steer that negative energy away from you.

Even more, if the stresses of his day are keeping him up at night to a point where you are concerned, making love to him can help him drift off to dreamland. His falling asleep soon after sex may be annoying at times, but if you understand the tendency, you can also use it to your advantage.

The main idea here is that, as you learn to be sensitive and recognize his emotional status, you will be able to minister love and support to him with the most powerful of the natural tools of ministry God has placed in his life... your body. This will also communicate your desire for his wholeness, you are there for him, and that you need him as much as he needs you. It prepares his heart to be open and receive things like spoken encouragement, prayer, and the

Word of God, which are emotional and spiritual tools of ministry.

PRINCIPLE ALERT

To further help you wrap your head around what I am saying, let me give you an image I believe you can relate to. Imagine your husband is like a car that runs better or worse depending on how much fuel is in the tank. This is because he has this intangible tank down inside of him that supplies his physical and emotional systems with the fuel he needs to function. Your physical love for him happens to be the fuel that he runs on, which means you are the only one who can fill his tank. You are the only one who has what he needs to handle life.

Now, if his tank is only about 10% full, he will be functioning on about 10% of his necessary daily requirements of confidence, motivation, and everything else that makes him go. His deflector plates that protect him from demonic thoughts and temptations will also be running at about 10% capacity.

When his **'love tank'** is full, his physiological status for the day is maximum drive and maximum impact. His deflector plates are at full power, and his temptation resistance is at its peak. He is primed and ready to face the world.

This is a simple example, but the love tank idea is a significant concept. You'll miss it, though, if you're still stuck on simplifying his primary need to be nothing more than a physical need to release (ejaculate). As we've already covered, the physical part of his need is just a part of it. He has an even stronger emotional need attached directly to it, and together, they are affected by how full his tank is.

So, for us guys, if our tank has run dry, not only will our physical bodies be screaming for attention, but emotionally we feel empty and unloved, like all life has left our life. Logically, we know our wife loves us, but we will feel like the only reason she does is because she has to. We see her as being driven entirely by duty rather than desire. This means she's not making a conscious choice to reciprocate, as we discussed earlier. She is just doing what needs to be done. The effect of which, as it pertains to passion, is about the same as tossing a wet blanket on a campfire.

The next idea here deals with the fact that the fuel level in his tank is constantly changing. As mentioned above, the fuel husbands burn to keep going is your supply of love and support in his tank. Like the gas in a car's tank, it gets used up, and at different rates depending on what he is working through. Quite obviously, if it is not replenished at a rate faster than it gets utilized, he will eventually run dry.

And there you have it, ladies. This is your husband's seemingly endless need for sex and physicality. It's as if he can never be satisfied... because he literally cannot be satisfied. It also means your physical love is much more of an ongoing emotional supply for him than it is a physical need.

Along with that, this is also why masturbation doesn't do the trick. Sure, a man can satisfy his physical need or desire to release, but simply ejaculating is not going to fill his tank. In fact, it usually has the opposite effect and runs it further dry. Only you, his wife, can fill that tank. You are the only one who can provide the substance of love and support that fills it and keeps it full. And as you all know, just like with your car, you must use the right kind of fuel.

PRINCIPLE #2

This area of choice versus duty is another place where we share the same basic programming. You girls have certain things you want your husband to recognize and do without being asked. You want them to be unsolicited expressions of his love for you. If you have to ask, it's just an act of duty. Not that fulfilling duty is a bad thing. It's just that when things are done for you that way, you can't help but feel he is only doing his minimum necessary requirements. He's not doing it for you because you are special to him but because that is what is expected... no more, no less. In other words, you would be able to logically conclude that he loves you, but only because he has to.

Now, if he does it of his own accord because he takes the time to notice and determine that you need this, suddenly it becomes an expression of his undying love for you. Not only would you be able to conclude that he loves you logically, but you would **feel** loved too... and that's where the portal to passion lies.

In the same way, your husband needs you to be sensitive to how full his tank is. If you make an effort to recognize it and do what is necessary to keep it full without him having to ask, beg, or even fight for it, your love goes from being a logical conclusion to something he feels.

Overall, it comes down to this. No woman wants to have to say, **"Tell me I'm beautiful. Tell me you love me."** It shouldn't be a fight to feel loved. We men need to endeavor never to let our love for our wives fall back to being nothing more than a logical conclusion. Be proactive in ministering to her heart... It's the portal to passion.

Likewise, no man wants to have to beg for sex and physicality. It shouldn't be a fight to feel loved. You ladies need to endeavor never to let your love for him fall back to being nothing more than a logical conclusion. Be proactive to keep his tank full... It's the portal to passion.

OK, one last thing before moving on. Developing this kind of sensitivity typically takes some time. This stuff doesn't come naturally to either men or women.

This means we both need to be patient with each other as we learn and develop these skills. There is no need to get upset and hurt because you had to ask for something. From your spouse's position, their love for you most likely had nothing to do with it. It simply meant they just missed it or didn't think of whatever it was ... probably because it wasn't something they would typically have been paying attention to anyway. In other words, it was nothing personal.

It's perfectly OK if you need to ask. And if necessary, ask again. Be thankful when your stuff does get taken care of. Eventually, they'll get it and be able to do those things in a way that makes you feel more loved by it... And that'll hopefully be right around the time you figure out how to do it right for them.

See? You love each other. You're OK.

That being said, I would like to revisit the dietary association I brought up in the girls' section. The meaty, muscle-building protein of your man's relational diet is sex, and all those activities that directly tie to the bedroom. The fruits and vegetables, which are equally as necessary to his overall health, are the physical things that happen outside the bedroom. It's the touches, the kisses, the adventures together... all those panties-in-the-briefcase types of things that round out his necessary daily requirements. This is why thinking men need sex may be true, but entirely incomplete. He needs all the different types of physical affirmations, just like he needs food from all the various food groups.

Sometimes we humans can get so focused on what we consider the most essential stuff that we forget about everything else. But don't be deceived. Without fruits and vegetables, protein can't do what it is supposed to do in us. Therefore, even though it may seem like certain elements are more necessary than others, each and every one is equally as important as the next. So, as difficult as it may seem, when communicating proper love to our spouses, we don't want to leave anything out.

Before moving on, I would like to address a stereotype that affects you ladies. It is somewhat of a theme to think that some of the activities listed above would make you feel like a prostitute. The reason why is simple. It is because those are the kinds of things prostitutes do.

This is a widespread and very real perversion of truth. The devil uses this to keep married women from feeling free enough to effectively love their husbands. As true as this misconception may seem, it is still a lie. You are under no obligation to allow such a thing to control your feelings and keep you bound.

First, a prostitute uses her body to do sexual things in exchange for money, goods, or services... to pay rent, get food, pay bills, have a car, have a place to stay, protection, etc. These ladies are supporting themselves through this practice, and many of them do it because they feel like it's their only legitimate option.

You, on the other hand, are not even remotely close to being in that same situation. These things you do for your husband are not to procure some payment, goods, or services from him. It is for the sole purpose of expressing your love for him and feeding his passionate love for you. It is all about strengthening the bond between you. The two purposes are monumentally different from each other.

Also, how many prostitute/client relationships have you seen where the two parties have committed their lives to each other, literally till death do they part? Once again, these two conditions are polar opposites. The relationship makes the difference.

Ladies, the devil is a liar. To live by his perversion would be perverted. Your marriage is sacred, sanctified, and undefiled before the Lord. Doing things that strengthen the bonds between you and your husband is absolutely the will of God. Be free to love him with your whole self. It's God's design, not the devil's playground.

I have a good example of what I am talking about. You can decide on your own whether you think this wife was behaving like a prostitute. Personally, I think she is one of the smartest women I've never met. I knew of her through her husband, a man I worked with on a jobsite many years ago.

He told me one day how much he hated, loathed, and despised painting. He hated it so much that he would rather pump sewage than paint a wall. His friends and family, already knew not to ask him for help because he would flatly refuse... even his own mother.

"But", he said, "Coincidentally, as much as I hate painting, I love doing it at home!"

I said, *"What?!"*

He said, *"Oh yeah. I love painting at my house. Because of how I feel about it, my wife already knows the only way she's going to get me to paint is if we do it together, and that's where it gets good. For some crazy reason, and for as long as I've known her, whenever my wife paints, she likes to paint in her underwear. It's true. The only thing she ever wears is a pair of panties and one of my older button-up shirts. It's absolutely amazing. I could just stand there and watch her all day, but then I get in trouble for not doing anything, so I have to get busy too. I love it! I still don't ever ask to paint anything, but I never pass up the opportunity to do it either!"*

So, ladies, what do you think? Was this woman acting like a prostitute or not?

You see, she was able to get her husband to do something for her that he very outspokenly despised. She accomplished it by letting her body do the talking. She was happy. He was happy. Their relationship was happy. Was that bad?

SIDE NOTE: This is for you guys. We have a propensity for going too far when it comes to sex and physicality. Because of this, I want to offer you a grave warning. If your sweetheart starts to open up to you in some of these ways, which are naturally very uncomfortable for her, you had better not gorge yourself on her goodness. Be intensely respectful and sensitive to her, as these kinds of things can make her feel particularly insecure. Remember that nonsexual affections are a big part of what ministers to her, yet here she is trying to do physical things for you. If she starts feeling like you are taking advantage of her efforts, you could ruin the safe environment you are supposed to be providing. If that happens, she will no longer go there.

In other words, she needs to know that she can let her body talk to you without having to be dragged up to the bedroom every time, or pressured into some activity she is not comfortable with. She also needs to know you are equally willing to go that extra mile to love her in her language.

You must treat her right because her Father watches out for His daughters. And you don't want to mess with that Guy because *"even the wind and the waves obey Him!"* (Mark 4:41). So, enjoy the moments when she blesses you with them and be thankful she is willing to light your fire. Learn to be sensitive to her so you'll know when it's alright to release the flames.

Before finishing this **little** section about the guys, I want to help put two and two together for you girls. Notice what I have been saying here. When your husband feels that physical connection with you, it fills him with confidence, fills him with motivation, causes him to feel supported, and makes him feel loved, etc. Notice how every one of the things your husband is ultimately in pursuit of is the fulfillment of an emotional need.

This means, believe it or not, that your husband's drive to be physical and his hyper-infatuation with your body is him being emotional. It looks and feels like the exact opposite from the perspective of female English, but when you peel back the surface level physicality of it, the thing that is driving him is a need to feel... to feel whole, to feel connected, to feel supported, to feel loved like I just stated.

It can even be more confusing because most of us guys don't even recognize it ourselves. We know we love sex and playing with your body. We get into all that physical stuff so much that we fail to see the reason why. This is especially true for those men who are so wrapped up in their hard-core manliness that they see themselves as too tough to feel.

But make no mistake. As I've been saying, God has hard-wired us guys in this way, so physical expression is how we show our emotions outwardly and receive emotions inwardly. These physical expressions are what connect our hearts to you and the world around us. And again, it is acutely different from the way you connect. The emotional expressions of your heart are a caring look, a gentle touch, and many meaningful conversations. It's why so many of you carry the stigma of loving to talk so much. Well, you're supposed to. It's how you are made.

Suffice it to say, for those of you who wish your husband would be better at, or more willing, to express his feelings to you, take heart because he already is. You just have to understand the language he is using to express them.

An astute woman will learn more about how her husband feels by how he is touching her, instead of what he is telling her.

So, like with the guys, there is a reason why you ladies should be willing to go beyond what is naturally comfortable to you and love your husband with spirit, soul, and especially your body. It's one of the most effective ways to feed and foster passion in your husband's heart. It's how you protect and strengthen your relationship with him. This is how you *let no man put asunder what God has joined together ..."*

♥ And Back to Both ♥

If you haven't picked up on it yet, please let me clarify. Many times men and women look like polar opposites because of the way they naturally function. However, the beauty of this is, the differences in our internal wiring create this perfect dynamic that God had envisioned when He separated male from female. When incorporating the whole of what we are and why we are, you find that we are not made to be opposites for the sake of being opposite. We are made to complement each other, to fill in each other's gaps, if you will, more than any other thing on earth ever could.

The trick is, that the only way to access the functionality of this powerful dynamic is to humble yourself. You must be willing to go beyond that natural drive to fix those opposite ways in your spouse. Natural minds think naturally. So, it's acceptable to believe that both of you need to think and act more alike in order to function in greater unity with each other. But by God's design, this isn't necessarily true. That spouse of yours doesn't necessarily need to be **'fixed'** so you can get where you need to go.

Once again, humility is key. Be willing to accept that you need to change your thoughts and beliefs about the differences between you. Be willing to accept that all their opposite wrongness is probably your fulfilled wholeness. Be willing to go beyond what makes you comfortable so you can minister to the needs that heal you both. That is how to start learning how to utilize this amazing dynamic the way God intended it to be.

This is a faith walk of agape. You are putting your faith in God, trusting that as you humbly bring your supply, His original design will work for you. You are choosing to trust that all those differences are not negative problems but relational benefits. You are humbly placing yourself in His care as you endeavor to give unconditionally to your spouse. It's putting your relationship first, by faith.

There it is, folks. So go fill your hearts with the Word of God and your cups with coffee, grab each other by the hand and go make some love... in all the different ways your hearts give and receive love.

So, let's review. Your relationship is your number one priority. The strength and support you need to tackle your everyday life come from that relationship.

Because it is a relationship between two people, it has two main priorities... his biggest need and her biggest need.

Husbands, you work hard to establish a stable and secure home and atmosphere for your wife to abide in. You develop yourself in the art of sexless lovemaking. Show her she is connected to your heart... her way. She needs that security. She needs to feel your love.

Wives, you shower your husband with your Femininity. You let your body do the talking. Show him you are connected and desire to be with him... in his language. He needs that security. He needs to feel your love.

One could say it like this. It would be foolish for a woman to believe God for a loving husband if she's not willing to accept the responsibility for loving her husband. Equally, it would be foolish for a man to expect a loving wife if he's not willing to accept the kind of responsibility necessary for loving his wife.

Together, you apply understanding and patience with each other. Communicate with each other. Pray with each other. Love each other. Your relationship is your focus, so feed it with the things that make it strong and healthy. Feed the need ... fuel the passion!

That being said, let's do a reality check. We can all acknowledge that this is not the one and only thing that makes a marriage work. Relationships can be very complex and multifaceted. They require total commitment by every party involved because they are built on things like trust, communication, sensitivity, and connection.

The things I'm sharing with you here are foundational to the structure of your marriage relationship. These things are focused on establishing your love firmly in place and then maintaining its strength and freshness. Developing yourselves in these areas will foster trust and encourage open communication. Surprisingly enough, if you are genuinely committed to your relationship first, you will actually grow closer as friends, than you do as lovers. I'm talking about the kind of friends who call each other every day to talk. The kind that goes places to hang out together. The kind that enjoys a good sleepover. More importantly, you will develop into a friend that your lover can fight the bad, celebrate the good, and live the rest of their life with.

But will doing these things fix all your problems? No, probably not. They will, however, help you keep yourself fresh and clear so you can deal with your issues rationally. Instead of getting the idea that this stuff is the end-all answer to your problems, think instead that it is the beginning of all.

Beyond that, not every woman and not every man is the same. We are generally not that far from what I've shared, but there are those, for whatever reason, where things couldn't be more different.

For instance, if you are married to someone who went through physical abuse growing up, you may very well be married to a person whose emotional make-up has been altered, due to what they have been through. Other people may have had a parent die way too young, or a disease, or something tragic beyond their control. Others may have come through great hardship or abandonment. Yet others have been bad people themselves and deal with a lot of guilt and shame. Even if you've never had anything horrible happen to you, sometimes you'll still go through challenging circumstances that alter your needs base for specific periods of time.

The reality is that, regardless of your particular situation, it is essential to remain flexible and be willing to adjust with your spouse. This will require ongoing, live-stream communication with them and God. Your love for each other stays relevant when it grows with them, changes with them, bends, twists, and turns with them, while you're both working through the challenges of life together.

Then there are cases where maybe you or your spouse are just made a little differently than typical. Perhaps you are that woman who naturally needs your nookie way more than your husband does. If this is you, be very understanding with him. He has a special kind of grace working over his life that is a mind-blowing irritation to the rest of us!

Whatever your circumstance, always be thankful for the one God gave to you. No matter how normal, altered, odd, or just different you or your spouse may be, you have something to treasure if you're willing to adapt. Hold fast to this truth because **strength to a relationship is protection for that relationship,** no matter who the participants are.

Let me help even further by reminding you that the person you are married to is God's answer to your prayer. If you are not willing to be thankful for the way He answered this prayer, you don't have much of a right to complain about how any of your other prayers work out. That's all I'm going to say about that.

Well, morning glory and hallelujah, commander! We have finished talking about what to do. Next, we will examine what may happen if we, for whatever reason, choose to ignore our spouse's most significant need. So, let's continue.

♥ *What if I don't?* ♥

"What if I don't want to do it? What's the big deal?"

This is the million-dollar question, isn't it? There is no denying the fact that as mere human beings, no matter how good we get at doing everything perfectly, we're still going to mess up and hurt each other's feelings. We are going to tick each other off and just plain blow it like no one else can.

So why try? Why waste so much energy on a lost cause?

You're more than welcome to think that way if you like. I'm not even bothered by it. You see, I am not trying to convince you to do something you don't want to do. I fully understand that life is unpredictable and that doing everything perfectly doesn't guarantee success.

What I am trying to do is help you position yourselves so when you royally burn each other's britches, you don't end up walking away like so many others have done.

Let's be real about it. There are a lot of married couples out there who seem to be getting along just fine without all that extra effort. A good number of them look like they are enjoying plenty enough success already. So why change? It's like the old mantra says, **"If it ain't broke, don't fix it."**

Well, personally, I am of the opinion that the kind of success we've had in the body of Christ, here where the power of God and presence of the Holy Spirit are free and available any time we call, is abysmal at best. How can we be where we are with that much firepower at our disposal?

Let Michelangelo explain it for me... he said, *"The greatest danger for most of us is not that our aim is too high and we miss it, but that it is too low and we reach it."*

You see, God designed your marriage to be awesome. But until we humble ourselves and work with the ways He made us, we will never discover how wonderful He intended it to be.

The truth is you are the way you were made to be. Whether you believe that or not doesn't matter. Until you put in the work to develop and grow, you and your spouse are going to function according to your nature naturally. So, let's look at it. What is the predominant response we humans have when our spouses, for whatever reason, ignore the kind of responsibility it takes to meet our greatest need?

It's simple, really. A person who is not getting their needs met will almost always try to do it for themselves. And keep in mind, at the beginning, this is not a function of spite. It is 100% a response to an actual, legitimate need not being taken care of. Desires are optional but needs are not.

It's like this. Hungry people eat. If your caretaker is not providing food for you, you will find a way to get some. It is a legitimate need in your life.

For women, if her husband won't take care of her, she will. She will typically become very independent and will work very hard to handle things on her own. She will shy away from anything that forces her to depend on him because down on her insides, she can't trust him.

Now, I am not against women being strong and able to take care of themselves but being independent is not how God designed married people to function. He made us interdependent upon each other, not independent of each other. We are supposed to be leaning on and trusting each other instead of protecting ourselves from each other.

Another common characteristic of women who are not being taken care of is that they like to be in control. I think this happens more subconsciously than anything because most of the time, she doesn't recognize it when she is being that way. Nonetheless, this stigma always seems to carry negative connotations about her, when in fact it could have been a man who caused it in the first place.

Many times, when you run into a controlling woman, you can trace this behavior back to an atmospheric deficiency. Somewhere along the line, the secure, loving environment she needed to live in was not provided for her. As I stated earlier, she was made to thrive within that atmosphere, but she was not made to provide it for herself.

Whether this deficiency began after she got married or if it was present while she was growing up, if she feels the need to take matters into her own hands, she will do so to the best of her ability. This requires taking charge anywhere she can and doing whatever is necessary to oversee everything that could impact her security. Again, this is often a response to an atmospheric deficiency, not a prideful refusal to be submissive to her husband.

Not only that, but a woman in this position will inevitably end up outside the protective covering that a marriage covenant would typically provide. She is vulnerable to situations where a different man could show up and illegitimately start ministering to the very need she is working to fulfill. And we all know where that story ends.

Men, if you have any desire to keep your wife's heart at home, then provide it for her. Give her the confidence she needs by loving her in the language that speaks to her the loudest. Be proactive. Talk to her. Give yourself to live attentively to her needs and work hard to provide them. You don't have to be perfect. You just need to be real. Be sincere and genuinely care. It's that simple (noting that simple and easy are not the same). If you do, you might have a wife for life!

For us men, if our wives aren't attentive to what we need, or if she makes it a big struggle all the time, we will do just like the girls and take care of it ourselves. This can manifest in several different ways. It'll show up through an over-infatuation with hobbies, constantly doing things on the side, or pretty much anything that lets us be up, out, and away. Men with a weaker moral center may even turn to prostitutes, mistresses, or actual affairs. For most men, though, it manifests through pornography.

Now look. We all know that porn is a massive problem in this day and age, and I am not going to suggest that anything here justifies it in any way. I will say, however, that before you ladies get too judgmental on the men for their disgusting, perverted issues, consider that maybe his little problem could be a natural response to a very real and legitimate need that is not being handled properly at home. Perhaps he's dealing with the same kind of atmospheric deficiency that drives you to want to take control all the time.

Along with that, when a man's love tank stays empty or almost empty most of the time, he will tend to be very insecure in his marriage. He will not be very confident that she truly loves him and wants to stay. This is a significant concern due to the fragility of his ego.

Men in this position tend to become very clingy, which typically includes a hyper-infatuation with sex. If your husband is regularly like this, chances are pretty good he doesn't feel very secure in your love for him. He's trying to fill his tank by latching onto you in any way he can.

This deficiency will also show up at work. These men can become so focused on making up for their own perceived deficiencies that they continuously end up shooting themselves in the foot. It seems as if something always happens to make their life more difficult than it needs to be.

And then, just like with the women, when a man is caught up in providing for his own needs in this way, he also will typically end up outside the realm of protection. He is vulnerable to some other woman conveniently showing up at just the right time, with just the proper attire, saying just the right things. I'll let you fill in the rest.

Ultimately, this is not what he wants, but as we all know, desperate people do desperate things.

Ladies, it comes down to this. If you want to keep your husband's heart at home, give him the confidence he needs at home by loving him in the language that speaks the loudest to him. Make him so full of your love that when some other opportunity or temptation tries to present itself, he doesn't have any more room in his tank. Keep him full.

You see, even though all those other couples out there may look like they're getting along just fine, you don't know what kind of resolve is tempered into their relationship. If the devil can convince you that you are just fine doing things the way everyone else is doing them, then he knows that if he hits you strategically, just the right way at just the right time, he can mess you up. You could end up like all those other couples you see getting along just fine without all the extra effort... whose marital success rate is less than 50%. Do you like those odds?

My heart, in presenting all these things is to help you do whatever you can do to shore up your defenses. You don't need help staying together when everything is going great, but you need great strength to stay together when, at just the right time with just the right circumstance, you experience the absolute pressure of the times we live. Choosing to change your perspective is up to you.

Let me remind you again. I have met a lot of people in my life who have admittedly divorced someone they still loved. I have yet to meet a single person who divorced someone they were passionately in love with. That is a 100% success rate amongst the people I have seen in life who feed passion into their marriage. Do you like those odds?

So, there you have it. The best way to hold your spouse's heart at home is to **feed the need.** Don't fight it. Be willing to humble yourself and shoot for the moon. After all, your greatest danger is that you set your sight too low and reach it.

♥ *Purpose* ♥

In this discussion about sex and sexuality, I would like to share some other interesting things I have learned over the years that should motivate you to re-categorize it in your minds. Fair warning, it may still be a little challenging for you to accept sex for anything other than how you already see it. Just open your heart and allow Holy Spirit to "**infect yer brain!**"

Remember, everything God does is for a reason, and there is a purpose for everything He has made. In that, we're going to revisit the devil's perversion about sex being only for pleasure and reproduction (something I will call **'the perversion'** from here on out). We need to get it burned into our brains that sex for human beings is different than sex for animals. It's not the same.

So, here comes a well-known fact about people. Our minds, our adorable human brains, love to categorize everything in our lives. It's what we do.

With men, it's really easy because in our brains, every individual piece of life and data is stored in its own special box anyway. Yes ladies. You have your very own box in there called the Wife box... right next to the Mouthwash box, the Lingerie box, and the Scented Heating Massage Oil that Tastes Like Cherries box. You are there right in the middle of it all. And your box is, of course, the biggest box we have because of how important you are to us (did you see what I did there?).

And then in you ladies' brains, everything is connected to absolutely everything. Still, though things may seem quite a bit more convoluted in there, the same thing happens. It is most particular as it relates to essential or recurring things.

For example, my wife has a very typical woman's brain that I simply cannot navigate my way through. But even so, she is a whiz at tracking things like spending. She knows where the dollars belong and what part of the budget pays for those trinkets I buy and all that wonderful stuff we call accounting. So, paying bills and keeping financial records is a categorizing function of her brain, yet all the while that whole concoction is somehow connected to absolutely everything else.

In-laws are a category. They are important and recurring people in her life. Children are, husbands are, and of course, sex is usually in a category by itself.

Thus, we end up with various categories in our brains that help us manage the different elements of our lives, much like folders on the hard drive of our computers. They help us keep everything in its place, organized, and in proper order by level of priority.

The challenge we now face, quite particularly because we're talking about sex, is that once a thing has been burned into a category, it is indelibly burned into that category. It is very difficult to think of that thing in any other way than what its original category depicts.

This is why first impressions are so important. Psychologically, re-categorizing a thing is not easy and can only be done intentionally. I think a few outstanding mind-altering drugs could be helpful, but you may end up with more of a mental potpourri, and that would be even more confusing.

So, leaving the drugs behind, the reason I'm saying this is because, as I stated earlier, in most of our brains, sex is in only two categories: pleasure and reproduction. This means that if you are feeling a little frisky, you either want some pleasure or you want to have a baby, or both. You can make up any other excuse you want for desiring sex but if there isn't a category backing up your claim, you are out of luck. It's either pleasure or making babies. You don't have other options.

Now look. Categorizing sex as being for these two things is not wrong. It's just incredibly limiting. It keeps your mind from allowing sex to ever be of any greater value to you than what pleasure and reproduction already are.

This is why it's a perversion. Sex should be a whole lot more to you and your spouse than just these two things. There are a lot of good reasons for having sex that go way beyond our two precious categories. For instance: sex is therapy, sex is exercise, sex is ministry to your soul, sex can be a statement to the heavens, sex can help you deal with stress, sex can even help you go to sleep to name a few. God made sex to have a positive impact on married people in many different ways. We typically don't explore them because we've been so ingrained in seeing it only for pleasure and reproduction.

It's unfortunate because sex is the trifecta of awesomeness. With it, you can accomplish something necessary, enjoy the pleasure of it, and build greater strength into your relationship all at the same time. To experience this, though, you will have to be willing to change how you view sex. See it more as a tool... that's great to use.

This is what I'm getting at. As necessary as it is for us to categorize all those things in our minds, if we lock those things into our categories, we can genuinely miss out on a lot of what God has for us in this life.

So then, with this being clarified, let me help you trick your brains into expanding the value sex has for you and your spouse. For starters, you will never realistically be able to remove sex from the Pleasure category. This is OK because it rightfully is a part of that category.

If you would like some scriptural proof, guess what! I have some!

Look at the story of Abraham and Sarah. They are both over 80 years old, which means Sarah has long since been through menopause... the rivers have run dry my friends. Then God comes to visit with a special message that the two of them are going to have a baby, and Sarah gets caught giggling.

OK now. Everybody always refers to Sarah laughing here because of the absurdity of an 80-plus-year-old woman getting pregnant and having a baby. Oh, nay nay! Sarah herself tells us why she was giggling in the 12th verse of Genesis 18. Read it and weep.

"Therefore Sarah laughed within herself, saying, 'After I have grown old, shall I have pleasure, my lord being old also?'"

O-o-oh Sarah! She wasn't laughing at the prospect of getting pregnant. She wasn't even laughing about having sex. Sarah was giggling because she was going to have sex and like it! She was giggling because Abraham was going to turn her on again. She was going to ... she was ... Oh, Sarah!

So, I think it's safe to leave sex right there in the Pleasure category. The trick is what you do next. You need to burn it into more categories. It'll be alright. If it's already in two, it can be in three, or four, or however many are necessary.

One way to accomplish this is never to allow your mind to end a thought or sentence with, **"sex is for pleasure"**. Always take it to the next step of reminding yourself, **"Sex is for pleasure, but it's also for..."** Then finish the statement with some other benefits of sex. Help your brain burn it into these other categories as well, so you can acknowledge and take broader advantage of what God has provided for you.

It sounds simple enough, but consistency is what makes it happen.

Therefore, based on what we have already talked about, **'Restoring Wholeness, Becoming One'** should become the most prominent category for sex. It is the beginning of it, the reasoning behind it, and the purpose for it. Think about that. Meditate on it and let it burn so intensely into your mind that it supersedes all the other categories. This addendum is the most important one.

Now, beyond that, let's get into the nuts and bolts of what other things sex can be. To start properly and on the same page, we're going to need to look at what real sex is, plain and simple. As we delve into this further, it's going to be essential for us to all start at the same basic understanding.

So then, technically speaking, if you, the husband, insert your penis into your wife's vagina, you are having sex. You don't even have to ejaculate for it to qualify. Throughout this book, though, let it be known that when I say the word sex, I am not talking about such a technicality. I am referring to mutually satisfying intercourse ... the kind of sex where you both experience storm-rated orgasms and lay there breathing heavy, sweat dripping off your skin and wondering what day of the week it is. If the bed isn't broken, the kids aren't utterly mortified by what they've been hearing, and you didn't have to run to the light, then it doesn't qualify! OK, maybe I'm exaggerating just a little, so we'll keep it simple.

Sex is mutually fulfilling, orgasm inducing intercourse.

Admittedly, there may be times when she is intentionally being a blessing to her husband by simply giving him her body. In which case, she may not experience much of an orgasm herself, but again, this would be an intentional moment, something she chose to do on purpose. And there may be times (for those who are strong enough) where the role is reversed and he is intentionally inducing her to orgasm without experiencing one himself. Again, this would be an intentional act of love, not the normal flow of lovemaking.

Along with that, you need to know that God built your body to produce orgasms when you are doing sex properly.

When I was investigating this material, I was shocked at some of the reports I saw of how many married women claim they seldom or never experience orgasm while having sex with their husbands. There is something seriously wrong with that.

Guys. If this is what it's like in your marriage, then if your wife lacks interest in a serious love life, it's just as much your fault as it is anyone else's. Come on, man! Just think about this for a minute, or two, or however many it takes to sink in. What woman in her right mind would ever actually desire to be taken away from her perfectly happy day/evening to go lie on a bed and get filled up with yet another mess to clean? For her to want something like that, it had better be worth it.

I'm just saying. You'll never convince me that that is what God had in mind when *male and female created He them*. No way. God has given you boys everything you need to fulfill your wife every time you make love, and none of it requires batteries. Care for her enough to learn how to be her lover instead of putting so much emphasis on being the head of her home.

I apologize for jumping onto a soapbox about it. I'm embarrassed that we as men have allowed ourselves to get so self-centered in our lovemaking. Don't ever allow yourself to be the only one enjoying an orgasm when you have sex. As a matter of fact, because of the way her body is built, if you're doing it right, she should be experiencing more than just one. The standard requires that if she doesn't get one, you don't get one, because if a man doesn't work, he doesn't eat.

Speaking of work, to make love by God's design, you can rest assured it's going to cost you something. You will both be giving effort, love, forgiveness, humility, vulnerability, passion ... and the list goes on. If you do it right, it'll expose you both to being as naked as you can be (spirit, soul, and body) and still wanting more. When that **'more'** happens is up to you, but there is an undeniable tug on your heart to be one with that person again. You can't help it.

Since sex is all about restoring wholeness, it is the quintessential representation of what intimacy is all about. You should be familiar with the **'whole person'** bonding that takes place. You sense it most at the peak of your erotic arousal, the climax of your passionate expression. In simpler, not-as-dramatic terminology, it's strongest when you both orgasm together.

So then, I believe we are all on the same page now. Qualified sex induces orgasms and is equally fulfilling for both persons.

Now with that clarified, let's get on the same page about what an orgasm is. God built your body with trigger points for systems that are all about inducing orgasms through sexual arousal. Since God obviously intended for them to be a part of your sexuality, and since most of you have probably never studied them out before, here is a brief explanation of what an orgasm is.

Orgasms are repeated, sudden, and charged emotional/physical surges in response to peaking waves of sexual arousal being induced by your lover. They are the height, the climax of your sexual encounters... when you are out of control and loving it. You girls will experience very pleasurable and satisfying contractions all through your vaginal region, and you guys will experience full ejaculation, which is the male version of the very same thing. Within the confines of marriage, this is where restoring wholeness manifests. This is where you feel intensely connected, completely one with each other.

Extramarital sexuality reduces this phenomenon to being not much more than a good time. Now, some may argue that it is a really good time, which makes it all worthwhile, but sorry. Not to bust your bubble or anything, but that isn't even in the same league as the real thing. When sex happens without a declared and executed lifelong commitment to each other, the deepest, most powerful part of this passionate uniting of heart and body is completely missing.

Within marriage, it is built on a lifelong commitment to each other. The covenant is the very thing that provides oxygen for your passion fires to burn. With that in place, the two shall become one. Without it, you are just burning with lust for each other, which is a watered-down perversion of the real thing.

So, with the **'what'** in place, I would like you to note that orgasms are supposed to be a very natural, very real part of married life. They are also effective for stoking the fires of passion in your relationship.

They are such a big deal, mind you, that the medical industry, universities, sexual advancement groups, doctors, psychologists, corporations, marketing companies, and even regular people like you and me have all conducted testing and experimentation to learn more about what they are, how they affect us, and why we love them so much.

I mean, since the church isn't interested, I guess somebody has to figure it out.

When you understand how orgasms affect your whole person, you see why sex that doesn't bring you both to orgasm is like buying a dozen eggs and then discovering someone sucked all the insides out.

Your marriage should give you life and vitality. Your love life plays a big part in that. God wasn't simply trying to provide married folk a little pleasure amongst the thorns by letting them have sex. He made it with a multitude of physical and emotional benefits to help bring His zoe life into yours. Orgasms are one of the tools He created to make that happen.

Physically speaking, they are good for you. A healthy orgasm can relieve stress, stabilize your heart, balance your blood pressure, loosen up specific muscle groups, give you energy, help you fall asleep, temporarily relieve pain, relax your whole body, start your period if something has caused it to be delayed, and even jump-start you in the morning if you're having trouble getting yourself moving.

A good orgasm will also reboot your brain. It'll fix those psychological bugs that were making your eyes twitch, just like turning your computer off and then back on again. It'll break down your pride, make you want to forgive, calm your mind (peace be unto you), give you positive thoughts, change your perspective, and it'll make your eyes sparkle because you are, and feel like you're in love.

Spiritually speaking, this is fantastic because a big part of becoming more like God (growing spiritually) is getting free from your own psycho-stuff. There is nothing like great sex to clear out all your mental clutter so you can focus on hearing from God better. Sex is not the only way to do this, of course, but it can be invaluable at times.

I haven't mentioned the fitness value yet. Let me tell you. When you do sex right, you are most definitely getting in some decent exercise.

There is an old saying that goes, "**If you do worship right, you don't need to go to the gym.**" I understand and agree with the fundamental truth of it, but worship isn't the only thing. Sex is right there also. Now it may not replace a whole-body fitness program, but it will most definitely give you a terrific workout... if you do it right.

Moving forward here, I'm not going to go into any personal details, but I can tell you this. Every one of the benefits I have listed above is something my wife and I have experienced at one time or another in our marriage, and some a bit more than others. And keep in mind, this is not a comprehensive list either.

There have been times when I would be full of negative, nervous energy for whatever reason, and was struggling to calm it down, or if later at night, get to sleep. One orgasm with my wife and poof. All that negative energy would drain away, and I'd be calm as a cucumber, and/or sleeping like a... well, sleeping anyway.

There have been other times when one or both of us were experiencing some pain in our bodies that was serious enough for medication. I'm sure many of you are familiar with that concept. Well, occasionally there would be times when we needed some relief while waiting for the drugs to kick in. Coincidentally, when you orgasm, your blood flow elevates because your heart is pumping faster. Plus, your system floods with endorphins, which, for a short period of time, will trick your brain into not recognizing the intensity of the pain signals being sent by your body. Thus, through careful orgasmic sexuality, we've been able to attain measurable relief from pain while helping to reduce the amount of time for the medication to take over. How's that for a handy tool?

And then there were other times, as I mentioned earlier, when we were on the brink of divorce or just not getting along very well. Throw some passionate love into the mix, and voilà. Suddenly, we could talk to each other, apologize to each other, forgive each other, and, most of all, love each other again.

Through opening our hearts and being willing to consider these things, we have ended up having, or you could say utilizing sex for many more reasons than what most would consider typical... and much of it with surprising results. Even though, as I've said before, it isn't the magic wonder pill that fixes every little wrong thing, we have still been thoroughly blessed by the multi-faceted way it has helped us to cope with, work through, and overcome them all. It's like a benefits package that comes attached to proper orgasmic sexuality, and it's just what Dr. God ordered.

Along with that, here's another interesting bit to think about. There are things that we do to ensure our spiritual health. There are other things we do to ensure our emotional health. Then there are things we do to ensure our physical health. All these things are different from each other because they address various parts of our being. Crazy as it may seem, a good healthy orgasmic romp in the sack is one of the few things you can do to bring positive change and health to all three areas at the same time.

In short, there are sometimes in life when you feel a little down, a little sore, nervous, or angry ... your heart's racing or maybe you just want to punch something. Sometimes you just need to feel close to your someone. God knew these things would happen from the beginning, so through providing a way to re-establish wholeness, He also provided an amazing way for us to deal with all these other challenges as well ... together as one.

So then, in summary, let's look at some of the different ways sex can prove to be that useful tool... that's great to use? Sex is for:

➢ becoming one again, restoring wholeness.
➢ pleasure
➢ reproduction.

- ➢ physical exercise
- ➢ rebooting your relationship.
- ➢ rebooting your brain
- ➢ helping you clear the clutter from your head.
- ➢ helping in conflict resolution.
- ➢ helping set the atmosphere.
- ➢ helping relieve stress.
- ➢ helping with pain relief.
- ➢ helping you go to sleep.
- ➢ helping you get going in the morning.
- ➢ uniting your minds and hearts together.
- ➢ helping establish peace.
- ➢ giving.
- ➢ intensifying your love for each other, infusing passion into your relationship.
- ➢ re-establishing perspective.
- ➢ showing the devil who's boss

Do you see? Orgasmic sex may not single-handedly fix every little thing you face in life, but it will help with so many of them. It serves a much greater purpose for your marriage than simple pleasure ever could. When you view and do sex by God's design, He works through it to help restore you to wholeness, healthy in your spirit, soul, and body. This is something I believe to have been His intention from the very beginning, when *"male and female created He them."*

Well, there it is. Sex! Here at the end, I hope you are able to see things a little clearer and in a more beneficial way than you did before. As we bring this chapter to a close, keep in mind that Holy Spirit is not afraid to talk about sex and sexual things. He will most definitely help to fill in any blanks you may have if you're willing to let Him. I know He would appreciate it if you gave Him that chance ...

"OK, Ma. Maybe that wasn't so bad as I thot it was gonna be."

... and of course, Bubbles

*T*o start, let me clarify a little about this chapter for you. It may seem to be a little more lighthearted, because it is. Even so, I believe it still contains great value in our endeavors to better understand each other. As you are reading you may find yourself asking, **"How on earth is this even important?"**, or **"Why do I need to know this?"**, or even, **"Where does this fit in the context of this book?"**

I get it, even before you get there. Don't worry though. It'll all work out for good in the end. Though you may not see the need or end up feeling a little unsure about it, remember that God read this before anybody else did and He still found a way to get it into your hands so you could read it too. It's OK. He's not embarrassed. As a matter of fact, sometimes I think He enjoys sharing things about subjects that make us uncomfortable. It's like He wants us to grow, to be more complete and well-rounded or something.

So then, are you ready?

Right here at the start, I will abandon the idea of standing on ceremony and get right to the truth. This word **'bubbles'** is nothing more than a less-invasive way of saying boobs, boobies, or for those of you who are of a more formal nature, breasts. Here-forth, whenever you see the word **bubbles**, you now know what it is referring to.

This chapter's general focus is for all you ladies out there who have been dumbfounded by us guys' seemingly uncontrollable infatuation with your bubbles. At some point in time, nearly every woman has asked herself or her friends, **"What on earth is the big deal with bubbles?! What is all the fuss about anyway?!"**

I understand your puzzlement. From your vantage point, bubbles are just a couple of extra appendages protruding from the front of your body. With the extra attention they need from you and the consistent ogling from men everywhere, they end up being more of a nuisance than anything else, especially if they're larger in size. And since bubbles are just parts of your overall anatomy, to you, they are literally nothing more than body parts. On top of that, it seems like the only time you use them for anything legitimate is when you have babies, which is generally a short period of time in your life.

Well, I can tell you, ladies, your bubbles are not just body parts. They are body parts... with style. I will show you why.

For you guys now, how many times have you heard this? **"What's wrong with you?! Why do you have to be so perverted? What's your problem?"** There's nothing like the sweet sounds of love and disgust. If you know this song well but have never been able to identify why you are the way you are, in reference to bubbles, I am here to help. Or if you have been frozen in sheer emotional terror as your wife corners you with questions about why you love her bubbles so much, yet not knowing how to answer because no matter what you say it will only make you look like a bigger pervert than you already do, this chapter is for you. Yes, my brothers. Have no fear, for I am here ... to help.

Now, again, I understand this subject may seem pointless to you if you are trying to learn some serious spiritual truth, but hang on and think about this for a minute.

When God made Eve, He did not take that rib out of Adam, start fiddling around with it, and in the process go, *"Oops! Didn't mean to do that! Hmmm. What are these? Oh, I guess that must have happened when I was pressing on the back here. Well, whatever. They're there now. I wonder what can we use them for ... Oh, I know. Brilliant! Bring on the babies!"*

Come on. I don't know anybody who could believe that God's design for Eve included an *"Oops!"* like that. This means that unless we can fit that little conversation, or one similar to it, into our doctrines of eternal truth, we're going to have to deal with the fact that God made bubbles the way He did on purpose. And that they are an essential part of you ladies' bodies with very unique and specialized functions. Then on top of that, He purposefully wired us guys to flip our noggins over them. In other words, your bubbles and your husband's love for them were the intentional work of the Most High, Holy, Righteous, Loving God of Glory and Eternity.

I mean, seriously. This concept will mess with your head, especially knowing that everything God does He does for a reason. And everything He has made was made for a purpose. What was He thinking?

I don't think any of us will have the complete picture of what He had in mind until we are there with Him and can ask face-to-face. Till then, He has given us quite a few pieces of evidence that we can draw from to gain a relatively accurate idea of what the concept could be. So then, let's take a look at some things we know:

- ➤ God designed and built Eve the way He did on purpose.
- ➤ God made bubbles as an integral part of the female body.
- ➤ God wired and programmed men to be drawn to those bubbles.
- ➤ God had a reason for making bubbles so mesmerizing to us guys.
- ➤ Based on this, He didn't create bubbles for the sole purpose of feeding their offspring.
- ➤ The more we learn about God's intent for what He has made and done, the more we understand His heart.

> ➤ The more we know His heart, the closer we get to living the way He intends for us to live.
> ➤ The closer we live in line with God's intentions, the greater the amount of His love and life that can flow to us and through us into this needy world.

So, in other words, learning about bubbles will help us win the world for Jesus! Ya-ay!

OK, so maybe bubbles are thankfully not a part of any real evangelism program but think about this for a minute. Have you ever wondered, or even noticed, why, of all of the amazing creatures God created in the earth, mankind is the only one where the males of the species go googly-eyed gaga over the baby-feeders on the females? We are literally the only ones.

There are many other creatures out there where the males will endure intense battles and crazy hardships just for the right to have sex, which doesn't seem all that far-fetched to us guys. It's pretty understandable, and for some of us, relatable. But you never see those other males creeping in behind their females to cop a feel or sneak a peek at her lady parts, ever. For some reason, they're just not interested in that part of her anatomy.

We, human males, are clearly in a class by ourselves. We are bubble lovers!

We have yet another interesting and distinguishable characteristic. Humans are the only recorded species where the female was taken out of the original form. Hmmm.

Now then, keep those thoughts churning in the back of your minds while we toddle off in a different direction for a little while. Let's clarify one of the main reasons why we guys can't ever seem to come up with a decent enough answer for you when you ask about your bubbles. It's because the honest answer covers quite a few layers of our existence, and we're not emotionally equipped to handle all of that at once, especially in the form of a simple explanation.

I was there too, but in my frustration, I decided to be brave and face it head-on. I took a moment to think about it as objectively and logically as possible. And then, when that quit working, I asked Holy Spirit to help me understand. It took a while, but with His help, I believe I have attained a logical way to explain this phenomenon. I hope this makes sense to you.

It starts with Femininity. Yes, it was the feminine part of the original Adam that was taken out to form Eve. Femininity is the principle thing that attracts us guys to you girls. It's the way you walk, the way you talk, the way you hold your head when you're thinking, and fiddle with your hair when you're bored. It's those silly little giggles and your tender touch. It's your curves and the way they move when you're just doing everyday things. It's the way you ask us to help you, and then it's those eyes... oh, those eyes... those stunning gorgeous eyes... those sparkling stars of the night glistening softly into the deepest corners of our souls ... oh, those, what? Wait a minute! Oh, sorry.

You see. The thing about you that draws us to you, like a magnet attracts metal, is Femininity. It calls to us, like deep calls unto deep. It draws us in like music from the Pied Piper's flute. And then, when we get close enough, your individual characteristics grab us and lock us in.

It all works very similar to a Venus Flytrap. It's pretty overpowered. It seriously is.

And please don't be offended by the reference. I mean, you girls are from Venus, right?

Well, here is something rather important about that. Both in physical form and by function, bubbles are the very purest outward expression of Femininity there is. They are the epitome of soft, warm, gentle, nurturing, inviting, sweet, and lovely. And with those shaping curves, who could ask for anything more?

Not only are they the purest expression of Femininity, but they grow out from the surface, on the outside of you, where they can be seen, held, and even interacted with. For us outside-in type people, this is like putting jet fuel in a muscle car. It's utterly fantastic because since bubbles are so purely feminine, we can see and touch the very part of us we've been desperately trying to restore since male-kind began. It's like finding the part we've been missing, the part that completes us.

When you think of it like that, why wouldn't we be head-over-heels for them?

That's not all, though. Their impact extends far beyond simple physical magnetism. It is also how they affect us from the inside out.

Yes. I did just say inside out, as opposed to the outside-in framework we men are known for.

Here is an example of what I mean. I'm about to be transparent about us men here, so please be kind, and don't judge us too harshly.

Our psyche is so intrinsically connected to our sex drive that if our love and bubble life is snagging up, we will literally have trouble thinking straight. We enter this state of pure emotional chaos. And if that's not hard enough to deal with, you girls can only see what's happening on the outside. The only way you can legitimately explain it is to conclude your husband is a grown man who is pouting, having an attitude, or acting like a baby because he's not getting what he wants.

I'm fairly certain that all of you ladies are almost entirely convinced of this about your man.

Well, allow me to expound for you. We are not pouting. Oh, nay nay! We are trying to remember who we are and where we come from. What is our mother's name? Where were we born? Did I ever know my father? Why is there a car in this garage? Why is it blue?

We are not having an attitude. We are dealing with an equipment failure that has caused a collapse of the circuitry that connects our processor to all our peripherals. Our memory cards are no longer communicating with the motherboard anymore, and the video drivers have somehow uninstalled themselves. I try to raise my arm to scratch my head, but end up kicking the door. This is a total meltdown here.

For us, this is no laughing matter. We hate this about ourselves. It's not fair that our sanity is directly connected to you and your precious bubbles. Especially when you consider that you, the woman God made for us to be that perfect and comparable companion. The one to spend the rest of our life with, isn't interested in dishing out sex and bubbles nearly as much as we feel we need them.

It makes me wonder if this wasn't the actual thorn in the flesh Paul talked about. Whether or not, let's give out a shout of praise to God for His grace that is sufficient in times like these.

It is a cruel fate that plays out generally undetected by you girls. To you, it's nothing more than a schoolyard temper tantrum by a spoiled little boy who didn't get his way.

I mean, the genius of this whole setup must be Divine. It's maddening with how dramatically we are affected down on the inside while looking like something so silly and immature on the outside. It's just not right.

No other person but God could have conceived that entire dynamic and made it happen so effectively. And even worse, I bet He thinks it's funny.

Nonetheless, as you can see, there are areas of life where we men are also affected, and very much respond from the inside out.

Now then, because of these things I've been sharing with you, let me say this. Ladies, you have no idea just how much power and influence you have over us. I mean, if you knew how to use your femininity properly, you'd be seriously dangerous. We would be utterly powerless before you... smitten and weak at the knees. You could get us to do almost anything you wanted, and we'd do it with a smile on our faces and a song in our hearts (refer to the most intelligent woman I've never met).

The accounts of this are not isolated or few-and-far-between. They are far-reaching and thread themselves back through the pages of human history. There have been countless men littered through time who have walked away from their deep-seated convictions or even direct commandments from God under the control of the mesmerizing gaze, the alluring way of a beautiful woman. This is some serious stuff.

If you don't believe me, take a good look at the seductress in Proverbs 7. First of all, it refers to the men who are her prey as **"simple,"** and I always thought this was hilarious because the word **'simple'** pretty much describes all of us.

Look at this scene here and what she does. She baits her male prey with a sense of adventure in that her husband is gone and shouldn't be back for a while. She tells him she wants his body (paraphrased) and then pulls out the ultimate weapon. She lets her body talk.

Don't think for one minute that kissing him was all about touching their lips together. It was a whole lot more about moving her body close to his, making sure he could feel her bubbles gently touching and rubbing on him while she touched her lips to his.

He was totally hooked (meaning he couldn't say no), and she could lead him anywhere she wanted, like a sheep to the slaughter.

So, here's a thought. God knew we guys would be defenseless against such a powerful thing, and that this weakness would cost us dearly, so why did He still make us that way?

Then let this blow your mind. The only thing this seductress was doing wrong was behaving this way outside of her marriage instead of inside it. She was doing what an intelligent wife does when she wants to motivate her husband.

God intentionally made us... Wait! Listen to this statement ladies. It is gravely true and may clear some seriously puzzling things up for you! OK. Here we go again. God intentionally made us men to be powerless against your womanly charms because He knew we would need a lot of help being motivated to do all the things you need us to do for you! You and your body are a big part of God's motivational program for men to love their wives properly.

It's normal to think he should be motivated all on his own, but how well is that working? As we have discussed, men are not going to naturally do everything you want or need them to do. And many of you already know, if you try to force him to do it, you're in for a rough time. Quite honestly, there is only one way that I know of (and I'm a man) to get consistent participation from a man to do things he doesn't feel like doing. You must find a way to get him to want to. So, ladies, of all the tools and equipment God has given you to work with, what do you think is powerful enough to get your husband to adjust his desires, to change what he wants, so he'll be willing to do what you need?

The only problem is, the devil has perverted this concept so much that a large portion of you married women won't tap into this power because it makes you feel like a prostitute, like the harlot in Proverbs 7. Go figure. The idea that God may have designed this dynamic to naturally function this way doesn't even cross your mind.

We talked about this prostitute mentality earlier, but it bears repeating. Ladies, this is 180 degrees out of focus. Married women are not acting like prostitutes when they use their feminine charm to motivate their husbands. In reality, prostitutes are the ones who are acting like married women. The reason they do it is because of how unbelievably effective it is on the men. It's great for business. They would be making a lot less money if they didn't. You see, the devil stole it so he could use it for his purposes and then perverted it so you wouldn't want to touch it.

This is where most of you say, *"But I'm a good girl, I am."*

Listen. The devil is a liar. When you desperately cling to this alleged holy position of ladyhood, you are yielding to his attempts to control you through your own feelings. Quit letting him do that. The battlefield is in your mind, so stop thinking that way. Defy him and go all sultry on your husband. Just see if he doesn't show up willing to do whatever you want him to do... because he wants what you've got cooking.

Remember Esau? He was so motivated **'in the moment'** by something as simple as food that he was willing to give up everything he had coming to him to get what Jacob was cooking. And now here you are, the woman of our dreams, holding the one thing we desperately crave the most. Using that very thing, you have the ability to cook up a stew thousands of times more potent than Jacob's paltry dish. Come on, girls. If Esau, a rugged and tempered man of war and the hunt couldn't resist giving all his future for some food while he was in the moment, how much more do you think your hunk-of-a-husband would be willing to give for a taste of you, in the moment?

Here, do this. On, say, a Thursday evening, sneak off and undo a couple of your buttons so M'Ladies can breathe a little. Then go to him and lean into him on the couch (or wherever he is) so he can see what you've done. Kiss him a few times on his neck and cheek while caressing his chest and then softly speak into his ear, *"I don't have the time or energy for you right now, my sweet, but if you can get the screens on the porch fixed by six o-clock Saturday evening I think I just might lose control of myself and make you wanna thank God for letting you be a man... if you know what I mean."* Then give him a little nibble on the ear and make your way back to what you were doing. Graciously do NOT give him any more sexuality than just that (because there is a good chance he might follow you). Have a plan and stick to your guns.

Come Saturday evening, you'll walk out to the porch and see the screens are fixed, walls are repainted, light fixture is cleaned, greenery hanging in the corner, got some fresh patio furniture to sit on, a new walk-out deck off the back door and a Jacuzzi installed to help you create the mood ... and there you are wondering how on earth he could get all of that done in just two days!!

"And prove Me now herewith saith the Lord of Hosts if I will not open you the windows of Heaven and ..." Oops! I'm sorry. I guess maybe that verse is talking about something else, maybe. OK. The point here is this. Don't blow this off, girls. This is me, a man, admitting something vital to you. How often does THAT happen? In so doing, I'm breaking the most cardinal rule of the Bro Code. I'm telling you our greatest weakness, which totally gives you the upper hand. On top of that, if you do it right, we don't even mind!

PRACTICAL SIDE NOTE: This will only be helpful to you if you're willing, but sometimes you're in a situation where you don't have the time for nookie, or you're not in a good place internally because of what you're dealing with. Still, your husband keeps leaning on you for some action. Well, because bubbles are one of the most effective ways to fill his love tank, you can literally 'tide him over' by giving him some interaction and a promise that when things clear up you will let him finish what you're starting. By lovingly communicating to him where you are at emotionally, and then investing a few minutes of 'bubble time', you can buy yourself several hours, or sometimes even days, if necessary, of peace from sexual pressure while you deal with the matters at hand. Just make sure you fulfill your promise when things clear up

Now I understand this goes entirely against the whole **"He should just understand where I am and respect me because he loves me!"** idea. And yes, ideally, he should. But realistically, how many men are at that place yet? We may understand the concept, but most of us lack the kind of fortitude it takes to pull it off. We know we need to grow strong enough to support our wives in times like these. But we are not quite there yet. This suggestion is not about feeding that weakness. It is all about working with what you have to get the peace and support you need while facing the matters at hand.

It's similar to driving on the interstate. When you have a crazy person riding right up on your butt and refusing to back off, you have a choice. You can get upset and start venting, spitefully locking him in behind you as long as you possibly can in an attempt to hold him accountable for being such a jerk. Or you can just let him get around you as quickly as possible and wave goodbye to all that stress and anxiety as it disappears into the horizon... before it steals your joy.

It's all about working with what you presently have available to maintain your peace. At the least, it's something to think about, anyway, if you're willing.

OK then. In the next step of our journey, I'm going to list off several things that are happening inside of us guys when we interact with your bubbles. This includes seeing, touching or whatever. This is the gold you girls have been looking for and the help you guys have needed all this time.

Before I do, I would like to say that this list came from the time I spent thinking, praying, and searching. I really wanted to know why I am the way I am, along with all my brothers out there. Like my other lists, it most assuredly is not comprehensive, but it does cover the basics rather well.

Of course, some of you men may not agree with my conclusions. I'm OK with that. This is the observation of one simple man in his attempt to answer this one elusive question that has puzzled the minds and hearts of women for centuries. I do believe many of you will relate to my findings. Then, you will be able to confirm for your wife what things are true for you.

Before diving in, it is of critical importance that I point out one more thing. The true effects of this list come out of a lifelong commitment to our wives. Just like with orgasms, men who go after bubbles without this covenant commitment never get past the physical pleasure of them. Though it may feel nice in the moment, it is still only surface-level pleasure. The depth and strength that is there to be had gets watered down and washed away in a sea of lust and selfish desire. If continued, it'll get to a point where the man doesn't even recognize the actual value of a woman or her bubbles anymore. Unfortunately, this places him significantly behind on the learning curve when he actually gets married, which typically creates other interesting challenges they will need to work through as they grow together.

Suffice to say, it's not worth jumping in the pool before the water is in it. You are much better off being patient and doing it right. Our passionate drive for oneness is not supposed to be misinterpreted as a passionate drive for sex and bubbles. It is believed to bring us to that place in our hearts where we are willing to commit ourselves to that one woman for the rest of our lives... only then obtaining the restoration and wholeness sex and bubbles are for. Fix your focus on that!

It's a lot easier to understand when you see that bubbles, like sex, were not made for pleasure, even though pleasure is a product of the experience. Bubbles are a part of restoring wholeness. They are all about giving and nurturing life.

Ok then. Here we go, ladies. When we, your adoring husbands see, touch, or interact with your bubbles in those special ways only you can truly appreciate, it has this effect on us. It:

- makes us feel close or connected to you.
- helps us focus because it eliminates all the other distractions around us.
- comforts us... especially when we are upset, sad, or stressed.
- invokes trust in us toward you.
- makes us feel safe.
- fills our love tank
- gives us drive.
- gives us purpose.
- gives us hope.
- gives us confidence.

- inspires our creativity.
- reminds us of who our one and only is.
- eliminates any interest in other women before it even starts.
- turns us on... makes us want you and only you.
- makes us want to turn you on ... be a better lover for you.
- makes us feel protected, as if you're not going to let anything come along and take us from you.
- makes us feel honored, because we are the only ones you allow to be there.
- makes us feel like we can conquer the world.
- makes us feel fulfilled and happy.
- makes us feel thankful.
- makes us feel pleasure.
- reminds us of why we do what we do.
- makes us feel deeper in love with you.
- makes us want to do nice things for you.
- makes us want to be a better man for you.
- make us feel content and satisfied, as if the world is a nice place to be.

How's that for **'inner sanctuary'**?

There are so many different ways we are affected by your bubbles, and they're all happening at the same time. This may not be such a big deal for you girls because you never have less than 10 or 20 things running through your brain at any given moment of any given day anyway. However, for us guys, this is a complete overload. I mean, everything on the list is emotional. Did you catch that? It's way too much for us to handle, yet we can't get enough. And don't ask us to explain it because we don't know how, as you may have already discovered.

That's why when you do ask us why we love your bubbles so much, we pause and think, stutter a little, and then start talking about how they look and feel. It's the only thing we think we can explain clearly enough not to cause any more confusion. But then, of course, this only solidifies for you girls that we must only have one thing on our minds.

Well, it's not that we only have one thing on our minds. It's that we have so many individual things on our minds that are all about one main idea, so we can't focus on any one thing... like watching a school of fish. And because we are not equipped to handle such a scrum, we don't know how to put it all into a simple answer that you can willingly accept without getting upset and removing our bubble privileges.

So aside from those cliché responses of being soft, and round and full, they're voluptuous, or they fit perfectly in my hand, or they're the only part of your body that's made to suck on, or they're so pretty I live for every chance I get to see them, etc.... There really are much deeper reasons why we are not just attracted to, but drawn to your bubbles.

And as you can probably figure out by now, those reasons come directly from our main original drive. We are driven to be one again... outside-in. Bubbles are a focal point of our passion because they are such a pure expression of your Femininity, the part we need to be whole again. And even more, they are on the outside where we can take them and bring them in.

Now, one of the items on the list was **"eliminating any desire for another woman."** This is not necessarily something to be concerned about, but I would like to clarify it for you nonetheless.

As men, and being visually stimulated the way we are, many times the devil will try to tempt us with thoughts or images of other women. Sometimes he will even use living, breathing women to try to lure our attention away from you, but most of the time this scenario plays out in the realm of thoughts and imaginations, in our minds. When it does, a healthy dose of your bubbles annihilates those temptations before they even have a chance to take root in us. They can't hang against Bubble Power, and this is what that item on the list is talking about.

Essentially, you girls are one of the most potent weapons God has given us guys to deal with temptation. When the devil tries to draw us away, spiritually we must speak the Word, but then in the natural we can run to you and let you and/or your bubbles do what they do best. All those things on the list are activated, and they serve to re-establish our heart for you and you alone. It declares to the heavens God's divine order and the true purity of our hearts. It's one of the physical ways we *"submit therefore unto God and resist the devil..."* as we are taught in James 4:7.

♥ The Destination ♥

Here we are, starting to descend before making our final approach. I'd like to look at a few thoughts on the way.

Bubbles are a Divine work of pure art, or otherwise, a pure work of Divine art. They are so powerful that they have moved more men on this earth than all the ships, planes, trains, and automobiles combined. This phenomenon happens because God, yes God, our Holy Father Himself made bubbles to be what they are and do what they do in us. They are an integral part of His design to motivate husbands, bring restoration and wholeness to you both, and strengthen your marriage by fostering your passions for each other.

Bubbles are also the only part of a woman's body that God commands husbands about in scripture. Proverbs 5:19

tells us: *"Let her breasts satisfy you at all times; And always be enraptured with her love."*

For those who are unfamiliar, the Hebrew word for "all" is indeed "**all**". So, to interpret that verse, it means we husbands are supposed to be satisfied with our wives' breasts, and enraptured in her love all the time. I didn't make that up. It came straight from the Holy Scriptures! And make no mistakes. It is no coincidence for God to infer that being enraptured in your love involves always being satisfied in your bubbles.

Ladies, don't ever despise your bubbles or your man's love for them. If you do, you are despising an integral part of how God intended to bring love and blessing into your life. Your Femininity and your willingness to let your husband partake of your Femininity are powerful tools to keep him motivated to be who you need him to be. It keeps his reason for endeavoring to be your everything plastered right in front of his eyes, **"at all times."**

Of course, you are probably thinking, "**He should do the things he needs to do because he loves me. Not because he wants my body.**"

You are not wrong, but remember. Because of the way God wired him, his connection with your physical body is what drives his love for you. It is the door that opens his heart. So, he is doing what he does for you because he loves you when he is being motivated by your physical appeal. As difficult as this may be to wrap your head around, it is still true.

Even more, I believe God loves this dynamic. He loves the way His male turned out. He loves the way His female turned out. He was the one who looked back over us and said, *"It is very good."*

In wrapping this up, let's go back once again and rehearse some of the things we know are true.

> - God made us to be the only males on earth to be drawn to our females' bubbles.
> - God also made us to be the only species with a will to choose, so we can live by the plan and design of Father instead of being led through life purely by animalistic instincts.
> - Then God made us the only species to have our Femininity taken out of our original form, leaving behind a male and a female. This separation set us on a lifelong passionate pursuit to be whole again
> - Therefore, we men cling to, reach out for, and are otherwise uncontrollably drawn to the part of us that was taken out, Femininity.
> - Bubbles, by natural structure and function, are the purest physical expression of Femininity here in the earth.

- ➢ Bubbles make us men feel whole again.
- ➢ Therefore, men cling to, reach out for, and are otherwise uncontrollably drawn to ... BUBBLES!

I'm not sure about you, but to me, this all seems a little too intentional. It's like it is all part of some divine design or something.

So, there you have it. The reason we men love bubbles as much as we do is because bubbles are the personification of that which makes us complete. It is why we are drawn to them and impacted by them in so many ways.

I hope this answer helps settle your mind. At the least, I hope it helps you understand a little more about the natural way we live with each other.

So, what about the spirit? Would God make something with as much emphasis and impact as bubbles and not have any spiritual value in it?

I don't think He would. I believe a biblical understanding of something as seemingly inconsequential as bubbles carry as much value to us spiritually as it does to our body and soul. Consider this for a moment. One of the names of God is El Shaddai, which carries more than one implication or meaning. One of these meanings is many breasted one. This is because the **"shad"** part of Shaddai is a root word that means **"breast."**

The concept is that El Shaddai is a giver of life, a nurturer, and a minister of wholeness... which describes the very function and impact breasts have on those being cared for by them.

Simply put, bubbles are a physical representation of the life-giving function of God.

Now take that understanding back to the examples we used from Genesis 1 and 2, where God formed man and then breathed His breath into him, and then in Ezekiel, when he prophesied to the dry bones who only came to life when the wind of breath blew into them.

We see that it is the breath of God that gives life.

This is significant because, as we have already established, we were made in His image and after His likeness. This means there are some characteristics that make us who we are that are common to both God and us.

Therefore, in the same way we men cling to, reach out for, and are otherwise uncontrollably drawn to Femininity (the part that was taken out of us to form woman, our bride), Jesus also clings to, reaches out for, and is otherwise uncontrollably drawn to His Breath, the part taken out of Him to form us (His bride).

You see, though men are affected by the weaknesses of the flesh, our love for bubbles comes from the same internal place as Jesus' love for us. It's a result of our drive to be whole again. Our human bodies are the temple of the Holy Spirit, you could say, the Breath of God personified. He abides in us. He gives us life, nurtures, and ministers wholeness to us like a mother nursing her child. We, as His bride, embody the very piece of Him that was removed to form us, and therefore are the object of His passionate pursuit for wholeness.

I believe one of the reasons the Bible uses the example of the Church as a Bride and Jesus as our Groom is that, like humans, Jesus would be drawn to what completes Him. Now, we may not have spiritual breasts, so to speak, but His breath, His Spirit in us has the same magnetic effect on Him that bubbles do on us men.

Jesus is as passionate about you as Adam was for Eve when he chose to give up everything to hold onto his woman. He stayed joined to her no matter what the cost to his past, present, or future. In like manner, Jesus was willing to give up everything to be joined to His bride.

In using a piece of Himself to create us, God secured our position next to His heart. We were made the object of His passionate pursuit of wholeness. We are complete in Him, and He is complete through us. It is an intimate, infallible bond like that which is between a Husband and His wife.

Now I'm sure some of you may be thinking that God is perfect the way He is and doesn't need us to complete Him. I would not disagree with you. Positionally, He is perfect. By His stature and position, He needs nothing. But relationally, He needs His companion. This need was why He created Adam in the first place. God obviously required a relationship with a comparable companion. Then, because He made Adam in His image, Adam needed one too.

If this concept is not quite sinking in, think of it like this. Even though God is all-powerful and can do anything, He still cannot do certain things. One of these things is lying. He cannot lie because He has chosen not to, and spoken it as His Word. Likewise, as it pertains to us, though God is all in all and could exist eternally of His own self, He still cannot live without us because He has chosen not to, and spoken it as His Word. Due to His own choice, He is relationally incomplete without you.

Added to that, being born by the womb is the legal entry into this physical realm. Therefore, He needs you in order to fill the earth with His love and life. You are a living portal between Heaven and this physical realm. The more we are connected with Him, the more of Him that abides in the Earth.

As we looked at in the very beginning, God chose to use a marriage, a husband-and-wife team, to carry out His vision here on earth. Therefore, we, the Church, are the bride and Jesus is the groom. Together we feed and foster our passions for each other and grow complete as one, to *"be fruitful and multiply, fill the earth and subdue it, and have dominion over every living thing that moves on the earth."* (Genesis 1:27).

See? I told you. Learning about bubbles will help us win the world for Jesus! Yay!

In actuality, you are probably wondering how on earth I came up with all that from something as eternally inconsequential as bubbles.

Well, the answer is simple. I asked Him. I asked Him to please show me what kind of spiritual validity we could draw from a subject like this.

Truthfully, I agree with those of you who may think writing a whole chapter about such a thing as bubbles is just silly and unnecessary. It's why I asked Him to justify, in a serious way, why He would inspire me to do such a thing. If He had a real reason, then what can we learn from it to help us be better brides for Jesus?

The next thing I know, it was almost like I could see Him, sitting there looking at me with this all-knowing grin on His face and saying, *"I thought you'd never ask!"* And the rest is history.

Now look. Through all of that, there is no need to get weird and try forming some silly doctrine of bubbles. Let's instead focus on being more thankful that this amazing God we serve cares so much for us that He can demonstrate His passionate love through the most trivial of things... things that don't appear to have any spiritual value whatsoever.

So go ahead and be free. Smile and giggle at the funny ways God made us. Enjoy each other to the full as you feed and foster your passions... but never ever forget that where truth meets reality, bubbles are not just body parts. They are not simply toys to play with, and are definitely not some inconsequential "*Oops*" that happened when God made Eve.

Bubbles and man's obsessive love for them are a demonstration of God's love for you. They are body parts ... with style!

DARES OLSON

Love Nuggets

I created this chapter to devote a little more time and attention to certain topics that I believe deserve it. These areas may not seem significant or important, but because of their impact on us individually and as a couple, I wanted to give them their own space and highlight them a bit.

Please remember that I am not trying to be your psychiatrist and most assuredly am not trying to disregard the value of a good doctor. These topics are deeply embedded in our nature, which is something God reveals to us frequently throughout Scripture and shows us through His Spirit. Because of this, I approach things from a pragmatic point of view, considering them to be basic, fundamental life knowledge.

With that being said, let me once again ask you to allow Holy Spirit's voice to be the one you hear. If anything here turns out to be something you deal with, then open up your heart and allow Him to form the words into the truth you need. My prayer is that what I say, or the way I say it, may be just the right touch to help you make the connection you need for freedom.

So here we go. Let me set the stage by re-stating some of the main ideas we have covered so far. **Passion** is the driving force of a fulfilling life. Relationally, passion binds us and keeps us together through anything and everything. **Sex** is about restoring wholeness, bringing that sense of completeness that has propelled us toward each other since male and female were first split apart. In the natural, a strong, healthy love life is one of the most powerful tools we have to keep our marriages strong and impenetrable to the devil's devices. As we give ourselves to making the kind of love our spouse needs most, we feed and foster the very passion that binds us together.

PRINCIPLE ALERT

Because we humans are so adaptive and resilient, we tend to lose sight of a little fact that ends up selling us way short of where we could or should be in life. That fact is this:
Survival is Not Success.

The only time survival is an actual success is when we are in a life-threatening situation. Beyond that, surviving something does not necessarily mean we were successful, that we did it right. It only means we survived.

Don't get me wrong. Survival is a good thing. Without it, we would all die. We need to adapt, focus, and persevere through our challenges, never giving up. The truth, though, will be told when we come out the other side. If we make it through a tough time in our lives but don't grow stronger as a person, if we don't experience more peace, joy, or confidence in the way God moves, we may have successfully survived that situation, but we were not entirely successful in it.

God made us all in such a way that when we hit rough waters, we are supposed to make it through to the other side AND come out of it in a better place than when we went in. It is not now, nor has it ever been, about simply surviving the storm, but about growing from faith to faith through the storm. It's all about coming out with more peace, more joy, more righteousness, a better car, a more productive job, stronger in body, more brilliant in mind, closer together, more confident with God, freer from fear, bigger in family, stronger in faith and overall, loving Jesus more than ever before.

Let's be real about this. For almost all the challenges we face in life, most of us already have an expectation that we will survive. It's like the understood **'you'** in a sentence. As tough as it may get, we still have this sense, this knowing that we are somehow going to make it through and keep on living.

Think of a small child who is learning to walk. Unless there is a severe mental or physical handicap, we all expect this child to learn how to get around on two feet. Nobody expects the child to fail and end up riding in a stroller for the rest of their life. And after they have successfully started walking, we don't glorify it and host an annual celebration commemorating the day our child defied all odds and overcame the unattainable by learning the art of walking. No. It's more along the lines of parents inviting family over to commemorate their child finally achieving what they were all waiting for, what they had been expecting from the very beginning. And if there is a party it only happens that one time.

In that, notice how this works exactly the way God intended. In making it through the challenge and struggle of learning to walk, this child has now put itself in a much better position in their life. Now they are stronger, more open to greater success, and more capable of achieving their goals in life. They have become a better person through it, and their life will never be the same as it was before the challenge started. This was more than just survival. This was success.

This example makes it very easy to see the value that is available through its achievement. It gives us a hint as to what may be there for us on the other side of the challenges we face now. This is important because as we grow older and face more challenges in life, our minds tend to draw conclusions by taking the path of least resistance.

In other words, here we are in our lovely little life, and Bam! A challenge hits us out of the blue, and now we are dealing with stuff. As expected, we make it through. In looking back, our minds tend to jump to the most straightforward conclusion and it usually sounds something like this: **"We made it. We must have done that right because if we didn't, we'd be dead or in a homeless shelter."** The problem is now set. For the rest of our lives, we think the right way to handle that kind of challenge is to do what we did then, but if all we did was survive, that's all we are ever going to do.

This type of experiential assessment is easy because it requires minimal effort, (the path of least resistance), but unfortunately, it is also a very inaccurate way to determine how successful you were. For example, If God was trying to work through this challenge to set you up for a better job, but all you did was make it through, it wasn't very successful. Or if He was working through it to get you connected to certain people or bring you a fresh perspective about a part of your life, and all you did was survive, it wasn't a very successful challenge for you.

In the arena of marriage, this principle is a vital truth to bear in mind. All marriages go through relational challenges that seem to threaten the bonds between us. Through these times, which can be some very intense fellowship, our responses determine the outcome. Many times, we are so glad to make it through that the steps we used to survive it become the principles of our future conflict resolution. Some couples become very skilled at quickly shutting things down because they struggle to handle the stress. With others, especially if you've been married a while, they will sometimes stop fighting simply because they don't feel like keeping it going. Peace and quiet are more important than winning the argument.

Well, as lovely as it is to rush to what makes your psyche comfortable, one question still needs to be faced. Where is the actual growth, the improvement into a better place than you were before? In other words, if you work through your challenges like this because you can't handle the conflict or want it quiet (or any other reason that is mainly focused on getting out of the storm as quickly as possible), then all you are doing is surviving. Nothing is being changed in a legitimate way to strengthen your relationship. Because you are focused on survival, your issue is more with the storm than it is with what's causing it.

Look. Again, let's be real about this. I grew up in a time when people stayed married come hell or high water. The bond of their word was a conviction that kept them from leaving, so they stuck it out. Unfortunately, I've met a lot of people over my years who had been married for very long periods of time but I would not consider their relationship to be a shining light or example of true success. Their commitment to each other forced them to stay together, so they learned how to survive, they figured out how to get along, and that's how their relationship worked until the end.

Survival, even if it's for very long periods of time, is still not success. Simply learning how to get along is not what God had in mind when *"male and female created He them."* Learning how to get along allows everyone involved to maintain their pride. It focuses on functionally working together in a way that creates the least amount of conflict. Relational success, on the other hand, is rooted in humility and selfless love. It requires everyone involved to lay down their pride and serve.

In other words, just because you and your spouse have successfully learned how to get along with each other doesn't mean you are experiencing a successful relationship. Your marriage is supposed to function like a superpower does for a hero. It's a total life hack that is supposed to bring you confidence, peace, joy, strength, and love. It's like that prized artifact every gamer wants that will boost your HP, buff your attack, give you a shield, and heal you in battle... if it's successful.

Through this very slight misrepresentation, the devil has successfully used our human nature against us for a very long time. And most of us have bought in because it flows naturally with the way we think and feel. To the extent that we don't even recognize it unless someone else points it out. Don't be deceived. This will sell you short.

All in all, survival is a good thing. We can develop qualities like perseverance and determination by making it through tough times. But never forget that survival is a horrible way to gauge how successful you have been, especially in marriage. As good as it may be, survival is not the same as success.

Now that we have this knowledge, let's explore some of these concepts and see what value we can derive from them.

♥ The Giving Supply ♥

This idea is a curious one for sure, and the principle behind it may be even more so than the words I've used to describe it.

I want to bring enlightenment to a longstanding idea that I believe is another perversion, so subtle our minds tend to blow right past it. Keep in mind now that when we are talking about a perversion, we are addressing something that is still a truth. It's just been tampered with, so by the time it manifests, it's usually far from or even opposite of what it should look like. And this little misdirection is usually all it takes to derail the train.

The perversion I am referencing here is thinking that giving and supplying are the same thing. They sound like they would mean essentially the same thing. The act of giving and the act of supplying appear to be nearly identical. So what's the big deal?

Enter the clichés, **"You're making a mountain out of a molehill."** Or, **"You're making the plain things into main things and the main things into plain things."** Or even, **"You can't see the forest because the trees are in your way."**

Well, the big deal here is human nature. The way we see a thing becomes the foundation for how our minds process around it. How we receive information, respond to, approach, or even handle life in reference to a thing comes from that foundation. If what we are seeing is slightly skewed, then our mental foundation will also be skewed. Even worse, if we are a little off, we hardly ever know it because everything appears right according to what we see.

Additionally, our human nature tends to gravitate toward the path of least resistance. One way we do this is how our minds naturally like to group like items and treat them as though they are the same. The justifying idea is that this requires less effort and is significantly more efficient in handling the various challenges we face in life. If the items are similar enough, what's the harm?

I'm not going to go so far as to determine whether or not this tendency is harmful, but I will say that it most definitely swings the door of misunderstanding wide open. With the varying degrees of severity and the many different ways misunderstandings negatively impact relationships, it would only seem prudent to avoid them as much as possible.

Now then. Bringing it down to the specific topic of giving and supplying, let's look at what makes them similar and what makes them different.

The thing that makes them similar is in the physical act of giving. In simple terms, giving a person is **'handing over'**, if you will, a gift to someone or something else. The act of supplying looks pretty much the same from the outside looking in. A person is handing over some form of supply to someone else.

The differences between them start with the items being given. Supplies are things needed to accomplish a greater purpose. Gifts range from things we need to things we want, things we like, or things we don't really care about.

The real difference, though, lies in the purpose, the goal of the giving, and most specifically, as it pertains to relationships. Another way of saying it is, what is the heart or motivation behind it? This is where it can turn into a really big deal because it impacts the giving and receiving of love between spouses. If the giving is done with the right heart and the right motivation, it becomes much more than just simple giving. It becomes a supply that is supposed to be the goal.

Here is a simple example to illustrate my point. The exact same scenario applies to giving in the offering at church. We see giving all over the Bible. Some more popular scriptures are Malachi 3:10 and Galatians 6:7, amongst many others. However, there are two that I would like us to look at in 2 Corinthians 9:7 and Ephesians 4:14-16. In the first one, we read that, *"... God loves a cheerful giver."* And in the latter we see, *"the whole body, joined and knit together by what every joint supplies, according to the effective working by which every part does its share, causes growth of the body for the edifying of itself in love."*

Notice that Jesus sets the Body in place, joining and knitting it together, not according to what each member gives to the body but by what each member supplies. One way to be a supplier is to give cheerfully. You see, each member brings more than just money or goods to a church. They have giftings and anointing to bring. When our attitudes are right before God, the gifts we give become more than simple giving. They also add to the corporate faith and anointing of that church body. However, if someone is giving out of a sense of obligation or begrudgingly, their gift may be nice, but it's just a gift. They are not adding to corporate faith or anointing because they aren't giving willingly or cheerfully. Additionally, they will likely not receive as much in the blessing department because their giving is not aligned with their spirit.

SIDE NOTE: On a short digression here, let me say this. If you personally struggle with the whole concept of giving and giving to the church, please do not feel guilt or condemnation. Each and every one of us is walking out our salvation with fear and trembling because we all have different areas in which we are still developing. In the previous paragraph, I am not trying to imply negative or condemning things over you because of where you are. I am actually speaking from a position that believes there are better things ahead for you, the more you grow in this area of life. It's OK to struggle. Just don't be satisfied to stay where you are. Keep your heart open and allow Holy Spirit to lead you through the good plan He has for you.

Alright, back on point. When you look at the greater effect giving with the right heart has, you can see that the giver is not only giving a gift but also supplying their part to the *"growth of the body for the edifying of itself in love."* And you can also see that if the giver is not giving from the right heart, they are only giving a gift. Although not a bad thing in and of itself, it is still limited to simple giving because it does not supply anything to the corporate faith or anointing of that church body.

So let's pop out of the church setting and into the other institution set here by God... marriage. In Chapter two, we talked about providing the thing your spouse needs most. Generally, women need a home, she needs that sense of security and she needs to talk. Most men, on the other hand, need consistent physical affirmation. Well, without going into all the details all over again, let's just suffice to say that when you give these things in the right spirit, you are supplying what your relationship needs. You are feeding and fostering the passions between you and thus contributing to the corporate growth of your union.

If you are giving these things but are doing it out of a sense of obligation or begrudgingly, you are simply giving a gift. The connection, that sense of wholeness, doesn't happen because giving with the wrong attitude stops short of being a supply. It may be a nice gift, but it doesn't contribute to the strengthening of the union.

That is the reason I wanted to shed a little light on this simple perversion. If we allow our brains to see giving and supplying as the same thing, then we are allowing ourselves the room to go through the motions of marriage. Simply going through the motions ends up not feeding or fostering anything but emptiness and division. And without some kind of intervention we all know where that road leads.

Here it is again. In the same way that we all need to develop the right heart for giving to the Lord, we also need to develop the right heart for giving to our spouses. This giving is supposed to be much more than just the gift itself. It is intended to provide the very thing our relationships need the most.

A simple way to gauge this is to look at what is accomplished by the gift. If it is appropriately given, it is supposed to make your spouse feel more connected and loved by you, the giver.

In other words, if you are a husband and you sit down at the table with your wife to give her a chance to talk to you about her day, the way you conduct your listening ear will have everything to do with whether or not she ends up feeling more connected and loved by you.

In the same light, if you are a wife and have agreed to some form of physical activity for your husband, the way you conduct yourself through that physical activity will have everything to do with whether or not he ends up feeling more connected and loved by you.

Too many times, we will go through all the right motions that qualify us for doing what we are supposed to do, while ignoring the intangible part of giving altogether. When you differentiate in your mind between giving and supplying, you realize that proper supply is accomplished through a physical act and an emotional connection. It's like the Spirit and the Word. We need both to accomplish the designed purpose. And too much of only one creates a problem.

Using a scripture verse we referenced earlier (Colossians 3:23) and melding it in with the ones we just used, we can construct a verse-like statement that solidifies the thought. *"In all you do, give it cheerfully unto your spouse, for the growth of your relationship and the strengthening of itself in love."*

So, back to our two little examples. If you are a husband and you have set yourself down at the table to give your wife a chance to talk to you, realize that you are not there just to give her some of your time and a set of ears to fill. You are there to supply her with a deeper connection, to make her feel more loved by you.

And if you are a wife who has agreed to some form of physical activity for your husband, realize that you are not there to simply give him your body and some of your time. You are there to supply him with a deeper connection, to make him feel more loved by you.

I believe this is an essential consideration because in order to experience the fullness of what God has in store for those who love Him we must endeavor to be the way He designed us to be. In our humanity, none of us is perfect in this. Sometimes we don't feel like doing it. For whatever reason, sometimes we are unable to meet the need. This is understandable, but it is still important to remember. Before you can act right, you have to learn to think right. So, please take this little section to heart.

I want to say one last thing about this before moving on. One of the fruits of developing this kind of heart is the freshness, the vibrancy of your relationship. When you and your spouse develop and function this way, it adds to the passion between you. This helps to keep things fresh and alive. No matter what age you are or how long you have been together, it still causes you to delight yourselves in each other, and that's a good thing. According to the Bible, we are supposed to, "... *rejoice with the wife of your youth ... And always be enraptured with her love.*" (Proverbs 5:18-19).

I think we can all agree that rejoicing and being enraptured are so much better than being blasé.

♥ Connection ♥

Interdependency is a thing... a very real thing.

I wanted to give a little extra time to this concept of interdependency. It is not co-dependency, although at times the two may look a lot alike. These are two very different conditions with altogether different effects on the relationship.

Interdependency is the intermingling of two hearts and lives into flowing and moving as one. Codependency is when a person attaches themselves to someone else because they either can't or don't want to function on their own.

The simplest way I know to explain it is this. It's like two people running a three-legged race together. For the two interdependent people, one will bind a leg to one of the other's legs. They will then work at and learn to function together as one, with three legs instead of four. Each is completely invested and entirely dependent on the other for their overall success based on how well they work together.

A co-dependent person is going to strap himself to the other's back and have them carry him through the course.

Now, granted, co-dependency occurs at varying degrees of severity, so my little example may be taking things to the extreme. Even so, this is still a straightforward way to see the difference between them.

If you are married, this idea of intermingled lives functioning as one life is like rebar in concrete. It's the internal reinforcement to the foundation your marriage is built on. Training your mind to think from this perspective can help eliminate many minor annoyances before they become significant problems. It should be one of your main relational goals.

I'll give you a fair warning, though. Some societies hate this kind of thinking. **"The voice of the individual must be heard. It doesn't matter whether you are married or not; you are your own person. You have your own dreams, your own desires. You choose your own path to show the world how great you and you alone can be. You are the only one who shapes your very own identity, and that identity is set on you alone. Finding your identity in anybody but you is weak and unstable."** And the rhetoric goes on and on and on...

Well, as it pertains to Christianity, Jesus laid it out as simply as it can be. He said, *"Or do you not know that ... you are not your own? For you were bought at a price; ..."* (1 Corinthians 6:19-20). Instead of you making your own way, Jesus already developed, built, bought and paid for an extraordinary destiny just for you. And that **'way'** is better than anything you could ever come up with on your own. You find your identity in fulfilling His plan, His will for you.

Likewise, a married couple is not made up of two isolated individuals who happened to live under the same roof with a contract granting them legal sex, shared insurance, and cheaper taxes. No. They are not there to live completely independent lives from each other. They are a man and a wife living out one life through two. Of course, there will be things they both do independently of each other, but even those are filtered through the unity they have between them.

Fiercely independent people struggle with this. Having to depend on someone else to grow, move forward, and get things done in life, goes against their grain. They generally believe adults should be able to take care of themselves. It's demeaning to think one would have to consult with someone else when they are fully capable of making logical decisions on their own.

Hey. Let's be honest. On the surface, their point of view sounds about right. But where's the heart of it? I ask because if this was true, what do we need God for? Is He only here for us after we die to give eternal life? I mean, seriously, if we can take care of ourselves, then we shouldn't need His help in order to live that more abundant life while here on earth. Am I right about it?

You see, no matter how adult you are, you still need Him. No matter how accomplished you may be at taking care of your own self, you still need Him. He brings things into your life that you cannot provide for yourself ... There it is! It ties right back to marriage because just like with Christ, your spouse brings things into your life that you cannot provide for yourself. You need each other.

God is the one who made marriage work that way from the very beginning, and He hasn't changed. This means doing the kinds of things that foster intimate unity with the person you are married to is not a weakness, but rather smart. Communicating with that other person and making your decisions accordingly is how it is supposed to be, as opposed to making sure everyone knows how adult you are.

In other words, unlike single individuals, if you are married, you don't have the right to go and do whatever you feel like doing because you feel like doing it. That other person's left leg is bonded to your right one, and you're both developing the ability to walk and run in sync with each other. Individual excursions don't work very well for very long without both persons being in agreement. Do you think that might be what Amos 3:3 is talking about?

I've been chided many times over the years because I'll be at the store and end up calling my wife to ask how she feels about me buying a thing (usually a more expensive thing, but not always). The ones doing the chiding are doing so because they think I'm a full-grown man who has to ask my wife for permission to buy something, much like a little boy would do with his mother. The fact is, though, permission isn't even a part of the equation. I want unity, and the only way to have that is for my wife to be in on it with me. If we talk about it, she can give me her input, and I can give mine. I am actually gauging how badly I want to pursue acquiring the thing in question based on the conversation I have with her.

Now, some of you may still think that's pretty weak, but I'm okay with that. I would much rather strive for unity than demonstrate my manliness by ignoring her and doing whatever the heck I want. After all, I'm a man and I can take care of myself. As a matter of fact, I can tell you right now that I am the man of my house (I can tell you because she gave me permission to say it).

It's easy and fun to be silly with the stereotypical male-female dynamic, but in the end, we have been given everything we need to think and act as one, the way Jesus and Father God are one. It is Jesus' prayer for the rest of us that we be one, the same way He is one with Father.

"And the glory which You gave Me I have given them, that they may be one just as We are one:" John 17:22

We can take this thought one step further. When we're doing marriage right, we are living right out in front of the world — a real-life, physical example of how Jesus loves His very own bride. In a big way, if we don't live in His kind of unity, the world will never see it.

Now then, because this is two individual yet interdependent parts of one, there is an extra dimension involved that is non-existent to co-dependency and hyper-individuality. As a husband or wife, you are an integral part of your spouse being able to overcome their weaknesses, succeed in their craft, and even walk out their salvation with fear and trembling. You play a role that is as critical to their natural life as God is to their spiritual life. I know this may sound odd, but it's true. Think about this.

In our three-legged race example, if one of the spouses keeps wandering their own way or tripping on nonsensical distractions, the other spouse will spend more time compensating and refocusing their attention than they will on actually advancing in the race. Or, if one of them actually falls or gets hurt, the way it is handled will have a dramatic impact on how quickly the fallen spouse is able to recover and get the two of them back on track to move forward again. Whatever the circumstance, or wherever each one is in their personal growth, when the two became one in holy matrimony, they together became one contestant in the race. They became dependent on what the other person is bringing to the table, along with their own efforts to move forward. No amount of spiritual prowess can compensate for the loss of impact due to a lack of togetherness between spouses.

In that, it becomes necessary to stop the brain train here. It's time to get off... and meditate for a moment.

We hear things like this three-legged race example and logically process what is being said. Through it, we can accept the word **'dependent'** because in our language, that is a word that fulfills the thought. It makes the whole idea make sense. But logical consent to a thought does not mean you are buying what's being sold. For this type of idea to make a difference in your life, it must transcend your logic and enter your reality; it must break free from the brain-train.

To accomplish this, take a good, hard look at what the word dependent means. While you're doing that, remember this little fact. The reason this word has the definition it has is because of the way it plays out in your everyday, physical, and very real life. It is describing a type of physical reality.

With real-life application as the foundation of the statement, you understand why we say the word dependent to explain the interaction between the two people making up one contestant in a three-legged race. It is because they, in a very physical and emotional way, depend on each other to compete in the race. In other words, this word is not used to bring clarity to the thought or idea being conveyed, but to describe the actual physical reality of what needs to happen.

A person cannot win a three-legged race by doing all the running themselves. No matter how slow or fast they may be on their own, they need their partner to run with them. Likewise, an individual who falls in a three-legged race cannot efficiently get back up and start running again without the cooperation and support of their partner. The fact that neither party can reach the finish line without the other's efforts means they are dependent on each other.

Taking this back to marriages, then, this means what it says. As a married person, the race you run called **'life'** is a three-legged race. In it, it doesn't matter how great you may have been at handling situations or climbing out of tough spots before, because now you can't do it alone. Now the rules for climbing out of those tough spots are different because you need someone else along with you in order to do it. Whatever situation you face, either collectively or individually, you need each other to successfully work through it. You can't do it alone.

This, as unpopular as it may seem, is the truth of it. This is what dependent means. Now, admittedly, there are varying degrees of dependency in its definition, but one thing you will find to be true. There is nothing in the overall concept of dependency that either means by definition, implies, or even indirectly hints towards somebody doing things on their own.

It makes total sense. How odd would it be for this all-knowing God to create something as monumental to life on earth as the marriage covenant and have the only area of literal dependency between the participants be offspring? I mean, beyond making babies, what do married people really need each other for anyway?

This is why it's so important to get off the brain train. When put in this kind of light, it is easy for all of our brains to agree that surely God must have intended for a man and a wife to be dependent upon each other for more than simple procreation. But if this is such a simple thing to see with logic, then just exactly where, what parts of us are supposed to be dependent on each other? And what is that dependency supposed to look like in everyday life? What was it that God had in mind?

You see, Jesus didn't even try to tackle His own life by Himself. He was the absolute and only person who could carry the sins of the world to the cross, but even though His assignment was incredibly specific to the individual, He still needed His Father to do it. At the same time, Father couldn't save the world without Jesus. They entirely depended on each other while doing everything they needed to do individually to fulfill the mission. They moved and flowed so interdependently that if you saw one, you saw the other. If you heard one, you heard the other. They were like the same person, even though they were two. It's no wonder Jesus liked to talk about His Father as much as He did, and Father talked so much about His Son.

This is what God had in mind. This is what you're choosing when you get married. You are accepting the responsibility to become a person who is so integral in the life of your spouse that they can't make it (succeed) without you. At the same time, you are also choosing to let your spouse become so integral to your own life that you cannot succeed without them. You are choosing to reshape your very identity from being the person your name used to identify, into being one who is an interwoven part of a union. You get reclassified as a husband or wife, the spouse of someone, instead of the stand-alone version of yourself.

It is essential to recognize that this version of dependency is a sacred bond before God, not the result of some psychological deficiency. It is the purest example of what a covenant is supposed to look like. Due to the diverse personality types and relational idiosyncrasies, there is no ideal, theoretically perfect way to walk this out. There is, however, an ideal attitude to have in approaching this kind of development. It is all about where your heart is. The Bible tells us that it is *"the willing and obedient who will eat the good of the land"* (Isaiah 1:19, paraphrased).

Another way of saying it is, *"Pride goes before destruction, and a haughty spirit before a fall."* (Proverbs 16:18). If you stubbornly hold fast to your own ways of doing 'self', resisting the idea of interdependency with God or your spouse you will end up experiencing the challenges in your life to a much greater degree than you should ever have to.

If you humble your heart and are willing to yield to His design, you will discover the difference between **'life'** and *"life more abundantly."*

I wanted to delve a little deeper into this subject because, in our day, the exaltation of the individual feels like the norm. Unfortunately, individuality is not what God had in mind when, *"male and female created He them."*

Getting your heart and mind right in this area can absolve a lot of strife before it starts. It will affect every part of your marriage from left to right, from top to bottom, from beginning to end. This will have an impact on how well you get along, how successful you are, how you raise your children, and even in your ability to fulfill the call of God on your life. It affects so much because it is yet another area where the exact same discipline it takes to be a good Christian for Jesus is also what it takes to be a good partner for your spouse.

SIDE NOTE: The most powerful, life-changing gift you can give your children is one voice. When they are young, this is even more impactful for them than the Word of God itself. This is because children who get one voice from both parents learn that true authority, God's kind of authority, can not be manipulated. This is critically important because it has a direct effect on whether or not they choose to listen and submit to the Word of God in their lives. Of course, once they have chosen to receive the Word, it will be the most essential, life-changing thing they have.

For parents, learning to function and flow as one is a crucial key. As stated earlier in this book, the strength of any people group lies in its ability to reproduce after its own kind. And I think we can all agree that making babies is only a small part of that.

Being willing to embrace interdependency and working hard to function in unity with each other not only gives your children the one voice they need but also gives them a crystal-clear picture of what it means to be a mommy and a daddy. It gives them an actual role model to emulate when they are faced with accepting their own role as a spouse and/or parent.

Additionally, it serves to train your children in the art of living this way. Their little eyes and ears are watching you and learning by your example more than anything else. As you live it, they live it. The next thing you know, you've got these young people who are out there carrying on the legacy through the lives they live as well. In other words, as a people, you are reproducing after your own kind.

Ultimately, it comes down to this. God made us to be interdependent upon each other. When we get married, we are no longer running the race of life as one person with two feet on the ground. We are also not running it as if we were two people with four feet on the ground. We are both, now, effectively running the race of life as one united person with three feet on the ground. The ground we gain and the time it takes us to get there are directly affected by how well we run as one.

Again, I understand this is not a popular message in today's world. The fact is, though, it doesn't matter how many hundreds, thousands, or even millions of people buy into the concept of individualism. The truth is still the truth, so don't be afraid to run this race as two interdependent pieces of one. Together you will *"walk as wise and not as fools, redeeming the time for the days are evil."* Together you *"... live and move and have your being ..."* Together you *"... walk by faith, not by sight."* Together you say *"I have fought the good fight, I have finished the race..."* As one, He will tell you, *"... Well done, good and faithful servant..."* (Ephesians 5:15-16 paraphrased) (Acts 17:28) (2Corinthians 5:7) (2Timothy 4:7) (Luke 19:17)

So let it be said, so let it be done.

♥ *Me... or not* ♥

Insecurity, it's a killer, sir. Yes, let's talk about insecurity, because it is a root-level issue that affects nearly every single thing you do in your life.

Looking at trees is the best way to understand what this means. If your life were a tree, you could deal with issues that appear on certain branches or limbs more easily because they are only affecting a specific part of the tree. Issues that are down in the roots, though, get soaked in and saturate the whole tree.

In other words, if a tree is growing in polluted soil, you will never be able to fix the tree until you cleanse the soil it is rooted in.

Human beings are remarkably resilient, though, and as a result have become very adept at living and surviving right along with our insecurities. Instead of cleansing them out so the tree, our life, can be healthy, we think it's easier to work with them. We'll simply adapt our lifestyles to function in a way that works around them. This gives us the ability to continue living mostly the way we like while avoiding our fears at the same time. We are so skilled at it that most of the time, we don't even consider these fears to be a big deal.

Unfortunately, though, fear-based insecurity is more like an iceberg. If you can see things happening out in the visible part of your life, you can rest assured there is a whole lot more going on beneath the surface, where you can't see it. As humans, the things we say and do, out where people can see and hear them, are the product of what we have going on down on the inside. It's why the Bible says, *"… out of the abundance of the heart the mouth speaks" and "For where your treasure is, there your heart will be also"* (Matthew 12:34 and Luke 12:34).

William Shakespeare even understood this when he coined the popular phrase, *"The eyes are the window to the soul."*

The concept is that a little bit of insecurity that is detectable to our consciousness is probably an indicator of a much larger, root-level issue down inside that is affecting a lot more of our lives than we are aware of. At the very least, these little insecurities deserve a more sincere approach to determining their source and how to address them.

Before we dive too deep, though, let me clarify something. Not all insecurity is fear-based control, or bad. Think of a virgin bride hiding in the bathroom on her wedding night. She is in there building up the courage to come out and let her new husband see her completely exposed for the very first time. It is pretty natural for her to be feeling a bit apprehensive. She is not being controlled by fear simply because she's feeling a little unsure about whether he will like or dislike what he is about to see. Because this is new to her, she doesn't know how he will respond, so those insecure feelings are to be expected.

It's very similar for a child going to their first day of school, or maybe their first day at a new school. Starting a new job or moving to the city when you were raised in the country are also examples of this. Essentially, when we are trying something new or for the first time, it is relatively common for insecurity to be more of a natural emotion than it is a fear controlling us. We know this because we still do it and become more proficient at it until we are no longer affected by it.

The flip side of this becomes the focal point of what we need to see here. If we can't overcome those normal feelings of insecurity, they can end up affecting us enough to change the way we live our lives. If this is you, there is most likely some kind of fear-based control that needs to be addressed.

In other words, if you have been married for several years but still struggle allowing your husband to see you naked, you probably have something more than natural insecurity affecting you. The same applies to each of the other examples as well, which conveniently brings us to a very important and essential truth about human life and relationships.

I think we can all agree that as Christians, and married couples, we should strive to function as closely as possible to the way God intended us to function. The closer we get to living His intended way, the more things work the way He designed them to work in our lives and relationships.

PRINCIPLE ALERT:

I apologize if this seems redundant. This is just too important to pass up. The truth revealed in this Alert can change your whole approach to life if you are willing to let the Holy Spirit work within you... if He hasn't already.

If you are a human being, when you are caught in one of the storms of life Jesus referred to as, **"trouble,"** you will find yourself in one of two groups of people. You are either a person who fights to get out of the storm as quickly as possible, or who is at peace going through the storm. You either believe that the storm is what is keeping you from peace, or that the Prince of Peace is there to help you develop your ability to have peace while going through the storm.

The storms in life are raging. Are you like the disciples, panicking and planning to die? Or are you like Jesus, sleeping in the back of the boat?

Let's dispense with any possible argument over which position is right or wrong. This type of discussion can never truly be settled because the disciples were utterly convinced that Jesus was being very irresponsible and not paying attention to the true issues at hand.

On the flip side, Jesus was thinking thoughts like, *"Why is it that you have no faith?!"* In His mind the disciples were being very irresponsible and not paying attention to the true issues at hand.

We need to approach it in this manner. The word Christian means Christ-like. It represents a person who is identifying themselves with Christ, not the disciples. This means that each of us who calls ourselves a Christian is endeavoring to become more like Him, and present ourselves to the world in the same manner in which He presented Himself.

In other words, if you are a Christian, then you are endeavoring to grow to a place where you can sleep in the back of the boat in the middle of a storm.

That being established, let me share a secret about Jesus and how He accomplished it. You see, Jesus left Heaven where He was Deity. The Bible tells us He *"humbled Himself and took on the form of man."* He entered this world through a physical womb and lived a physical life as a physical man.

Now I know this may come as a shock to some of you, but when Jesus lived here on earth, He did not have any superpowers. He couldn't shoot laser beams from his eyes or leap tall buildings with a single bound. He wasn't doing timey-wimey things, and He couldn't wave his hand around making all the naughty stuff disappear.

What made Jesus' life and ministry so powerful was how connected He was to the Spirit, who could.

If Jesus, the man, was here using cheat codes or superpowers, then how on earth could we as mere humans emulate Him or strive to be like Him? But if Jesus were here, functioning with the exact same limitations that we deal with, and was still able to accomplish the things He did, then we could learn from what He did and how He did it. Ultimately, we can then do the same things, or even greater.

In that lies the secret to the storm. Jesus was not intimidated by how big, bad, or mean any storm was. Because He was passionately connected to His Father and Holy Spirit, He wasn't afraid or worried about what the storm could do to Him or His future. He was free to go catch up on a little sleep, knowing it wouldn't have the slightest effect on the outcome of His life. He had already prepared for the absolute worst by strengthening His connection to the greater One inside. Then, when the storm hit, it was as if He already knew they would make it out OK, because He already knew they would make it out OK.

Most of us start like the disciples, though. We fully understand that in order for us to have peace, we need to get out of the storm. Get out of there as quickly as possible because the wind and waters are rough and dangerous. Outside the storm is where things are smooth and calm, so run from the racket to lay hold of your peace.

This mentality feels so natural that, in many ways, it defines the way we tackle life. It's how we think. It's what we believe ... but Jesus, who thinks differently than we do, came so we could have life and have it more abundantly.

One of the great things about a disciple is that the name itself implies growth and learning. A true disciple never stops changing into being more like the image of his/her master. As disciples of Christ, we strive to be more like Him every day.

Well, Jesus was not at all irresponsible in the middle of the storm. He was at total peace and was therefore able to think clearly, make solid decisions, and help others know what to do in the process of getting themselves through it. He wasn't fearfully jumping to conclusions and flailing about in a state of panic. Sleeping Jesus was the man with the plan.

So remember. In this world, there is going to be trouble... storms. You may think the best way to survive is to get out of the storm as quickly as possible, and you might be right. But survival is not success. Allow Holy Spirit to lead you and keep your eyes on Jesus because true success comes when you can peacefully sail through any water.

When you learn to see things this way, you gain confidence on your insides. It's like you know everything is going to be alright, because you know everything is going to be alright. Happy napping...

So let's tie all this back to insecurity and marriage.

Insecurity is a form of fear. It is a victimized pride that manifests in various ways in a person's behavior. Here are just a few of them:

> Insecure people have a hard time receiving genuine compliments. Many times, they either discredit them as disingenuous or misconstrue them as some form of insult.

> Insecure people will lie about what they want and hope someone will give it to them anyway.

> Insecure people will overcompensate their own lack of true confidence by being very controlling or arrogant.

> Insecure people either have an excuse for everything or blame it on someone else. They struggle facing themselves.

> Insecure people hide behind a skill or ability, or even a cause, that lets them disappear into the masses.

This list only has five items on it because I didn't want to take it any further. Trying to list all the potential effects would just be cumbersome and digressive.

I also stopped with these five because they seem to be fairly common manifestations of insecurity. I'm confident that each of you has dealt with people like this at some point in your life, so you are familiar with what I am saying.

Now these behaviors are not signs of imminent failure or death. In fact, people have become so proficient at constructing their lives around these things that they don't even realize it's not ordinary. In many cases, individuals can adapt and be quite successful in life while still harboring the insecurity that leads to these kinds of behaviors. The main idea I want you to see in it is found in answering this question. What kind of effect would these have on a marriage where a husband and wife are trying to develop intimacy, trust, and oneness with each other?

When you take a good, hard look at it, you see that insecurity can cause a person to behave in a way that is 180 degrees opposite of where their relationship should be heading. It's as if insecurity is a sworn enemy of intimacy, working very hard to prevent it from developing.

If you are an insecure person or deal with insecurity in different areas of your life, you should take this very seriously. You can't treat it like it's a watered-down, harmless version of the actual bad stuff. It needs to be treated like outright fear because unchecked insecurity will undermine everything your marriage is supposed to be built on.

With that being said, let's do a quick reality check. We are looking at some of the most natural hindrances in our lives. So natural, in fact, that many times we mistake them for legitimate parts of our personality, the things that make us who we are.

Don't be deceived. Those things you like or dislike, gravitate to or shun are all elements that help make up who you are, for sure, but fear is not one of them. Anything that grabs hold of you from your insides to control the way you live is not a part of your personality.

Another way of saying it is this. God did not create you to have your ability to live freely restricted by your personality.

"God has not given you a spirit of fear (insecurity), but of power and love and a sound mind." (paraphrased, 2 Timothy 1:7).

This is where we look to Jesus again. He prepared for the worst by connecting to the Greater One inside of Him. We prepare the same way. The more connected we get to Holy Spirit, the more we live in that righteousness, peace, and joy the apostle Paul wrote about.

This is significant because the Righteousness of God destroys insecurity! When you find your identity in Him, your own insufficient identity issues will start to disappear. Your confidence is no longer in yourself but in God, who is more than sufficient.

Now let's add a little marital magic to the recipe. As we have already covered, when you are married, you are no longer an individual with all your individual things that make you such a unique and wonderful individual. You are an interdependent part of a person who is made whole through the intimate connection between you and your spouse. Your relationship is where you are bonded and through it true oneness is formed. Remember, though, that this relationship is also a source of strength, life, and identity for you. So much so that drawing faith and security out of your marriage relationship will also cause things like fear and insecurity to begin to fall off naturally.

In other words, when you choose to feed and foster your passionate love for each other, you are infusing your relationship with power. This power diffuses any fruit of fear and insecurity that may exist in your heart. In that, you are not only doing your part to bind your hearts inseparably, but you are also helping eliminate the effects of the devil's previous work in your individual lives. You end up gaining confidence in each other instead of confidence in yourself. Just as with several other things we've mentioned, the qualities that make a good spouse are also the same qualities that make a good Christian.

One of the closest things we have in this natural realm to demonstrate God's perfect love for us is the pure, passionate love between a husband and wife. And it is no coincidence that both His love and our love work so similarly toward the same end for each person. A healthy marriage relationship will function like your relationship with God. They both work closely together to drive out things like guilt, shame, doubt, fear, insecurity, unbelief, and anything else the devil has worked so hard to seed into you. In an atmosphere enriched with this kind of love, there is freedom.

Let me remind you again. I understand that God is the source of life. All anyone, whether married or not, needs is Him, and they will be fine. I get it. Yet, God has chosen to bind His omniscient omnipotence to work only through His word. He is also the one who set up the union of a man with his wife to be His primary strategy for filling the earth with His love and power. It means He would have intended all along for this union to be a means of providing His life to His children. It's as if He wants us to be dependent on each other, to foster unity, just as He does.

This becomes particularly evident when you examine the numerous areas of a person's life that improve upon getting married. I'm not going to go into a bunch of statistics here, but things like being better adjusted, more able to cope with change, generally happier, better at problem solving, more successful, and even living longer lives are all advantages that come with being married. They all seem to just happen. The funny thing is that science can only understand why these kinds of things happen up to a point. The rest is just a phenomenon.

Well, it's not a phenomenon. It happens because God made it that way. He designed it so the marriage relationship would be an avenue to bring His life into our lives where we need it most. It only goes without saying that the more you strengthen and feed that relationship, the more of His life can flow through it.

With that, I would like to conclude this section on insecurity with a bit of encouragement. If you are dealing with insecurity in your life, like most of us, you do not need to feel guilty or ashamed. The motivation here is to help you understand that you don't want to treat it as if it's normal, as if it's OK to stay. I mean, it's generally considered normal to deal with sicknesses at different times in your life, too, but it is not normal for those sicknesses to stay in your body for the rest of your life. Neither illness nor insecurity allows you to function the way you were made to function. So, as normal as it may be to deal with such things, we still treat them for what they are, an enemy of health, and so we work to get rid of them.

I am also not saying that if you have insecurity, your marriage is doomed. I am saying that if you acknowledge and treat insecurity properly as a legitimate fear, you can deal with it appropriately, so it will not hinder your marriage.

It comes down to this. *"Fear God and keep His commandments."* *"... do not be afraid."* *"Be strong in the Lord and in the power of His might."* (Ecclesiastes 12:13, Matthew 14:27, Ephesians 6:10). As you are vigilant to deal with insecurity, God will be vigilant to support and guide you through it. Be free. The rewards of intimacy reach way beyond the cost of exterminating fear.

♥ *Abuse* ♥

This is a hot topic for a lot of couples because of the impact it either has or has had on their relationship. Therefore, I would like to put in a little effort to discuss it. Though I am not a doctor, I hope some of my basic observations will help you on your journey to personal and relational wholeness.

Before diving in, though, I would like to reiterate this idea. Marriage changes all the rules. It doesn't matter how long you may have been together, once you solidify your eternal commitment to each other, you have entered the point of no return. You have relinquished your escape routes, and now things are real. The way you relate to each other after marriage often changes from the way it was before. You are now spiritually, physically, and legally bound together for the rest of your lives... and that's different.

I'm saying it again. Getting married adds a whole new dimension to a person's existence. It can get quite challenging for any couple to work through and adapt to the new, different ways they need to function. Then, if one or both of them have endured something as life-altering as abuse in their past, the challenges can even multiply.

One obvious reason is this. Within the close and intimate confines of a marriage relationship, you can find love and strength, but you will also be exposed and vulnerable. Typically, abuse creates a powerful feeling that you need to protect yourself the most from the people you are the most vulnerable to. The only problem with this is that you can't grow closer together and protect yourselves from each other at the same time. Marriage is all about drawing close, which doesn't work well when one or both parties are used to handling life at an arm's length.

For those who have never had to deal with anything so invasive, it's usually much easier to be open and vulnerable with their husband/wife. For them, it's only natural to feel and expect that their loving spouse is just as committed to being open and vulnerable with them as they are. And that's when the fun starts.

Because of how different things get after the marriage, it's easy to imagine how a person with no abuse in their past could feel like somebody pulled a bait-and-switch on them with their spouse's personality. It appears as early as their first real challenge together, especially if that challenge was a result of a mistake they made. They go to their loving bride or husband for care, support, or even forgiveness as normal couples should in those moments. But instead of finding that faithful and loyal companion who is committed to stand alongside them through the thickest of evils, they find themselves staring down the nose of a fire-breathing dragon that is snarling and vaporizing everyone's happy thoughts. Then they realize they are the prime course on the menu.

"Oh my gosh! Who are you and what have you done with my snuggle bear?!"

For some of you, this may sound a bit overdramatic, but if you are the person in this scenario, you are most likely thinking, **"That pretty much says it like it is."** And that is when both people step back and start reassessing their decision-making paradigms.

It can also show up at the most inopportune moments, such as when making love. A movement can be made, or a specific something is said that instantly triggers memories...

memories of negative events from the past. Suddenly, your passionate lover disappears into a protective shell, and this highly erotic moment becomes very quiet and, many times, frustratingly awkward.

PRINCIPLE ALERT:

I would like to point out that animated, intense communication can still be effective. It may not look like what you think it should, but it can still be.

We have all heard for years the importance of effective communication, but many times we treat it like we do opportunity. It has been said that most people do not recognize opportunity when it comes knocking because it comes dressed in coveralls and looks too much like work.

In that same vein, most people don't recognize effective communication when it begins to happen because it comes right in your face and looks too much like strife.

Look. Intense communication is still communication. It may not look or feel like what our refined Christian selves think is acceptable, but if it helps get those bent up pains and suffering, those crippling fears, and the inner torment out from being bent up down inside, then Hallelujah and Praise the Lord!

Most of us have also heard the computer mantra, **"garbage in = garbage out,"** and how that principle applies to our hearts as well. Well, think about this. The situations that drove those overwhelming, gripping emotions down into you or your spouse's heart were not pretty. They were hard. They were stressful. They felt evil and full of malcontent. You could say they were... garbage in.

Well, if that's what they were like when being driven into their soul, just what do you expect them to look like when they come out? Are you expecting some kind of joyous event where sparkly angels gather around and gently flap their wings to the sound of happy songs filled with praise and sunshine? If that's what you think, please let me know how that works for you.

Oh nay nay! If you or your spouse is a human and all these things looked nasty and cruel when they went in, chances are pretty good that they are going to look nasty and vicious when they come out. You could say they are... garbage out.

Here's the kicker. If you both keep your hearts right, blasting out with this kind of intense communication won't make you a bad person... but it can make you free. That's right. Even though it doesn't look at all like good little Christians sharing every thought in words filled with love and harmony, it still performs the effectual work of drawing out the poison, the source of the suffering.

Surgery is not pretty, and healing hurts. If you truly want your life to get better after some form of trauma or injury, you need to be willing to endure a little ugliness and pain. True, effective communication is far less what it looks like and far more what it does.

Let me make this clear. I am not advocating fighting for the sake of fighting in your marriage. Fighting due to an overall lack of self-control is childish, and like Paul, when we become mature, we put away childish things. But when the events of your married life trigger negative responses due to past fears and pain, don't be afraid to be real. Be gut-level honest and forthright about how you are feeling. Fight the silence and draw out the poison. Don't let it retreat back to hide under its protective shell. And when it gets hot and crazy, go with it while keeping Genesis 2:25 at the forefront in your mind. This is one way you provide an environment for your spouse to be completely exposed, completely naked in. It's one where all the ugliness can be seen and dealt with, with no shame.

Don't worry about how God sees you both in that moment. He already understands that healing in humans rarely looks precious. He is much more interested in the results. He is the Spirit of Freedom, the Prince of Peace. For us humans, these two things never come without a fight.

Interestingly enough, when the hearts that are involved in something like this are pure, the other side of the battle tends to be even more passionate or fruitful than it was before things got started. This is especially true if it happens during intimacy. The heightened emotions and the release of all those frustrations charge the atmosphere. It can get so electric that when the smoke finally clears, it's all passion... raging fires and dancing volcanoes.

Again, true effective communication is much less what it looks like and way more what it does. Do you think God is unhappy with His kids when they blast their way through some gnarly emotional resistances and end up being engulfed in the fires of their passion for each other? I think not. It's through passion that love and healing do their best work.

The main point here is this. When triggers occur, it is more important to express them than to remain quiet and composed about it. Do not suppress those emotions to keep some form of peace. Be honest. Be frank. Be forthright. Even if it doesn't look or sound the way we think good Christian folk should sound, getting the poison out is a much higher priority.

So I'll say it one more time. Even animated and intense communication can still be effective.

Whether this explains your experience with intrinsic accuracy or you've experienced a more watered-down version of it, it's still time to go back to the basics and focus on what is essential. Let's dive into the main ideas of this section.

Right away, let's get one thing straight. Nobody is broken or flawed here. People who have been abused are not less than or of poorer quality than anyone else because of how they handle their life now. On the contrary, these people are the way they are because their psycho-emotional structure did what it was designed by God to do under the extreme circumstances they went through. And if those circumstances continued for any extended period of time, it is very natural for their adjustments to stick.

I have found that these people, though they may struggle with things like trust and intimacy (closeness), tend to be overachievers in many other parts of life. They live with a resolute commitment to life and are often times given to compassion. That is not broken or of lesser quality than anyone else. So whichever person you are in your marriage, you must still value your spouse's strengths and be willing to work through (notice I didn't say change) their weaknesses.

With that being said, if you are in this boat but have a desire for a healthy marriage, I believe there are some things to keep in mind that will help you as you sail those waters.

One of those things is this. If you have been through abuse in your life, you must be willing to accept/admit that the way you handle life and relationships is probably not the same as people who have not been through it. This difference will show even more when dealing with your spouse, and will likely create additional challenges as the two of you work and grow together.

Look. It's tough enough for any man and woman to learn to live together as it is. But when these types of differences are added to the mix, it just makes resolution that much more challenging. Don't go thinking that it's bad, though. It simply means you will both need more *"love, joy, peace, longsuffering, kindness, goodness, faithfulness, gentleness and self control."* (Gal. 5:22-23). How can that be bad?

Either way, as hard as these challenges may be to you, due to what you have been through, you must also consider how difficult dealing with this whole new set of parameters is on your spouse as well. If they came from an abuse-free environment, they are not at all used to dealing with someone who handles life the way you do. Their expectations for how you both deal with adversity are probably very different from what you are giving them. I mean, everybody knows that a mouse is primarily a docile creature. But a mouse will bite you in a nine-line second if it feels like you have backed it into a corner, like in the following scenario.

Your husband probably thought he was approaching a sweet little mouse who was willing to talk and air things out when you snarled and bit him before any words were even spoken. He's probably used to the snarling and biting coming after the peace talks have broken down, but you're not like that. You must assert your measure of offense-based (justified) dominance right off the bat so he knows just exactly how badly he can get hurt if he tries that again!

It's a silly little example, but surprisingly close to reality for a lot of people. And, of course, it could work that way for either gender.

Simply put, remembering that you are probably handling things like strife and misunderstanding in a way that is quite different from what your spouse is familiar with can help you be a little more understanding as you go through the process of growing and adapting to each other. You are not the only one having a difficult time.

Another thing to keep in mind is this. A big area that gets changed through abuse is the threat perception/self-preservation mechanism. It becomes almost entirely driven by emotion. This alone can create a lot of misunderstandings because in the world of emotions, perception trumps reality. Where logic has a finite set of parameters and protocols that define perception, emotions are intangible and therefore lack true definition. A person who is functioning from a platform of logic, who is trying to effectively communicate to a person whose platform is emotionally driven, is like trying to fly a kite from a submarine. I'm sure it can be done, but when it is, it looks very different from what we would consider normal.

This is important because, as we all know, unchecked emotions will go over the top and blow things way out of proportion. If you understand that your threat perception/self-preservation mechanism is driven by pure emotion, then you can also understand that the perceived threat you are responding to may not be as big and/or devastating as you think it is. What it feels like is often very different from how it is. Therefore, when it shows itself, you can cut your spouse a little slack, knowing their perspective isn't being driven by the same thing yours is. Again, nobody is wrong or broken; just different.

One thing that is most essential to remember, whichever side of the coin you are on, your spouse is still your biggest ally in life.

Now, here are a couple of things to keep in mind if you are the one married to someone who has been abused. We sometimes get this idea that because these abuses happened in the past, we should all be adults here and do like Paul said, *"forget those things which are behind and press for the mark for the prize of the high call of God."* (Phil. 3:14 paraphrased). Well, I'm sorry to bust your bubble, but most of the people who have been emotionally altered from abuse don't **'change back.'** This is the person they have become, and this is the person they are.

Now, of course, there is healing growth that comes with time and experience. And, of course, there is God who can and will wipe away the effects of past pain. But in the real-life, everyday humanity of it, that battle for self-protection never goes away.

It's easier to think of it like the Rapture. Whether or not you believe in the rapture is totally between you and God. However, among those who do, there are some who essentially stop investing in their future because they believe the rapture will occur before they can ever see a return. In reality, you are supposed to live your life still as if you'll never see it, even though you believe it could happen at any time.

In the same light, even though you still believe that God's Spirit and His Word will continue to work healing and restoration in your spouse, you live your everyday life as if you'll never see it. You can't hold out for some magical moment when they change back to functioning the way God originally intended. You must be willing to adjust and adapt how you do everyday life with them. Their healing/restoration is not required for you to live in unity.

Now, for you, great men and women of faith, this can get your undies all in a bunch. You feel like you are being forced to compromise your holy Christian principles to get along with this heathen person you're married to. Well, chill a little. Relax and fix your undies while you ask yourself this question.

What do you think God cares about more? Your well-developed holy Christian principles, or the unity between you and your spouse. As you contemplate your answer, consider the only prayer recorded in the Bible where Jesus prayed for us (John 17:20-26). He prayed that we would be one, just like He and Father are one.

You see, God is intrinsically more interested in the unity between both of you. The fruit of it far outweighs anything you could accomplish from your own spirituality. You must remember that both of you make up one contestant in a three-legged race called life. You can only make progress forward if you are working together.

Here is another thing to keep in mind. Most of the time, when your spouse is engaging in battle with you, it isn't because of how they feel about you as a person. They perceive a threat and are instantly driven to eliminate it by any means necessary. You may hear several things about who and what you are, especially if you are perceived to be part of the threat. You may even hear things about your parents and your upbringing. There is quite a wide array of things you might hear in the process of working through it, but in the end, it is all a bunch of protective froth and bubbles.

Your spouse loves you. If they didn't, they would not have married or stayed with you. It's easy to hear their words and see their demeanor and think they hate you, or at the very least are disappointed to be stuck with you. This is all rubbish. That whole display comes from an emotionally driven defense mechanism, not a heart. It's a reaction to a perceived threat. Behind the barrage of war-like behaviors and all those walls of protection is a tender heart seeking a safe, loving environment to abide in.

Do not try to understand your spouse's image of you from these emotional outbursts. We've already mentioned how the driving emotions behind them will blow everything out of proportion, including the things that are said and felt about you, **'in the moment.'** It's way too easy to get insecure in your love for each other over things like this, so guard your heart. Don't let the devil keep taking advantage of you in this area by being too moved by what you see. We walk by faith and not by sight.

Again, your spouse loves you. They are probably more committed to you than you are to them, even if they don't show it well. Chances are probably high that they are desperately trying to hold onto you on the inside.

Once again, I want to stress that nobody is broken here. The existence of extra relational challenges does not equal 'bad.' It is different, of course, but it is not bad. Humbly adjusting to each other's weaknesses to be able to work together is a primary function of relational physics, anyway. There should be no guilt or shame involved; instead, a simple, pragmatic approach to running this race together is perfectly fine with God.

I give you Ecclesiastes 3:11 to solidify the thought... *"He has made everything beautiful in its time."*

Hopefully, these little observations are helpful to you. Before finishing out this section, I wanted to talk on a broader scale, just a little. The things we face in our lives and marriages serve a larger purpose. Many times, they are also products of the devil's larger purpose, and that's what I would like to illuminate a bit. Sometimes it helps to know what is going on in the big picture.

Jesus told us in John 10:10, *"The thief does not come except to steal, and to kill, and to destroy..."*

This is also seen in Isaiah 14:13-14, where the devil reveals his master plan. *"For you have said in your heart: 'I will ascend into heaven, I will exalt my throne above the stars of God; I will also sit in the mount of the congregation on the farthest sides of the north; I will ascend above the heights of the clouds, I will be like the Most High.'"*

Humans are the only created beings made in the image and after the likeness of God. We were the only ones fashioned by His hands and brought to life by His own breath. And our bodies are the only ones to be designated as a temple for Holy Spirit to dwell in. It is no coincidence that God told Abraham that his offspring would be multiplied like the stars of heaven. In other words, humans can be likened unto the stars of God.

So basically, if the devil can exalt himself to a place of authority (exalting his throne) to where he can rule over mankind (the stars of God), he will be functioning like the Most High. In other words, he will be able to control God through controlling us. This is his master plan.

It's not a bad plan, as far as plans go. But it is still entirely insufficient and more of a last-ditch grasping-for-breath type effort because there is still no escaping the Word of the Lord.

Nonetheless, there it is. In walking out his plan, the devil needs to do anything he can to trip up, delay, or even stop each human from fulfilling the plan of God for their lives. He learned from the tower of Babel that the best way to do this is to destroy unity. If he can keep us functioning at an arm's length from each other (sounds familiar, doesn't it), then he will never have to worry about the anointing (his kryptonite) getting too strong on the earth.

In saying that, I believe you can already see where I'm going with this. It is always important to remember where your pain came from.

If you have suffered abuse, it came from the devil. He has a malicious plan to steal your ability to trust the people you need to trust the most. He wants to kill your desire to be one with God or your spouse. And he wants to destroy your ability to fulfill God's plan for you by getting you to be hyper-focused on yourself and your protections. If you take a good look around you, it is easy to see that abuse is a very effective tool in accomplishing this goal... and so he used it on you.

If you are married to someone who has been through abuse, you need to know that your spouse is not the only one whom the devil was after. This is especially true if you are farther down the path of spiritual growth than they are. When you buy the lies of what you see with your eyes instead of what you know in your heart about your spouse, you end up giving the devil a fantastic two-for-the-price-of-one deal that makes his efforts even more worthwhile. Now, if you add in the dysfunctional children you produce from the confusion and every evil work, his success keeps growing and growing.

Can you see the reaction chain here? By tripping one person up, over time, he is creating a whole line of people whom he doesn't need to concern himself with when things get real.

I want you to know that striving for peace, working for unity, goes way beyond your little selves. Of course, God wants you to be blessed in the lives you live now, but He also has plans that involve your children, your children's children, your brothers and sisters in Christ and beyond. Don't take this lightly. Pursue healing and restoration in your ability to trust your spouse with your whole self. Pursue your ability not to be moved by what you see but by the truth that resides within you. Fill your home and your relationship with the Spirit and the Word because the fruits of the Spirit are the very things God has given you to carry and protect you when the waters get rough. Fruits are healthy for you, so produce them and eat them up.

Finally, let me say this. Feeding and fostering your passions for each other also has an impact on this part of life. It helps to clarify your focus and keep your priorities in the right place. As I've said, it may not fix or eliminate all of your issues, but it can certainly help keep you bonded together while you work through them.

It comes down to this. From the fruits of the Spirit to passionate love, the Word of God, and the Spirit who guides us, He has given us potent tools to help us find peace and live in unity, no matter what you have been through. But like any tool, they don't do anything for you by themselves. You have to pick them up, and you have to engage yourself with thought and effort to use them. I pray you do because of what you can become when you live and act as one... *"Eye has not seen, nor ear heard, Nor have entered into the heart of man the things which God has prepared..."* (1Corinthians 2:9).

♥ *The M-word* ♥

Menopause. For many men, it doesn't matter how many letters you spell it with; it's still a four-letter word. It's more like **'men-on-pause'**.

Yes, many battles have been waged over the effects of this very thing. Some have even been so brutal that they ended up in divorce.

I believe it's heavily involved in a phenomenon we've seen in recent years, where people who have been married for 25, 30, or even more years suddenly end up getting divorced.

What on earth is that all about? You'd think after all those years together, they'd be set for life.

Generally speaking, we are told that these poor folks discovered they no longer love each other. They've drifted apart, and now they're not compatible. Since the kids are gone, their shared goal of raising the little sprites is now behind them, so the only thing left is just them, with no buffer.

Now I'm not speaking with undeniable proof here, but I do think it is rather coincidental that right around the time period when the kids are moving out coincides with the same period of time when menopause starts moving in. In other words, the timing of these breakups suggests that this condition may have been involved in a little more than just some physiological changes in the woman.

The deal is, when a woman goes through it, wonderful and horrible things happen. On the wonderful side, she doesn't have to deal with a period anymore. On the horrible side, a sadistically vicious desire-consuming demon monster appears and sucks out any and all of her want for sexual fulfillment.

It's a heartbreaking, truly devastating time for us husbands. Both of you are there having a perfectly lovely day when suddenly the skies begin to darken. Some thunder rolls, and the lights start to flicker. A black cloud begins passing through your house and engulfs your wife in its evil as it moves through. Then suddenly it's gone as quickly as it appeared, and there is your sweet little bride, looking as beautiful as ever with her lovely eyes sparkling at you. She gently smiles and says, **"What?"**

You don't know what, for sure, but you can tell something's not right. And then it shows itself. The next time you try to get frisky with her, she stops you on a dime and tells you to act your age ... **"You're not a teenager anymore, so get over it!"**

What? Where on earth did that come from?

Look. When your wife would rather go scrub the floors behind the washer and dryer than play patty-cake with you, you know there is something seriously wrong.

Don't laugh. This happens. Though it may not be quite as theatrical as I've made it out to be, it feels like that to us guys.

Unfortunately, menopause was never intended to be such a horrible thing. The problem we have run into, though, is the impact it has when mixed with the devil's perversion of sex, that it's only for pleasure and reproduction.

You see, as we've looked at earlier, **'the perversion'** affects the way love is given between a man and his wife.

It goes like this. Since making babies is off the table at this point in life, the only remaining reason for having sex is pleasure, much like the lollipop example from chapter two.

In this scenario, sex and sexual activities are nothing more than unnecessary luxuries, and since a person can survive without luxuries, sex is not necessary.

Therefore, Mr. Husband's so-called need for sex is not as legitimate a need as he would like to think it is. She is hooked into the real truth here, and he's just not willing to admit it yet.

That's unfortunate, for obvious reasons.

Why? Because since this sex is for nothing more than pleasure, and now she has very little interest in that sort of luxury, he's pretty much going to get left out hanging with the wash. She's going to tell him he needs to grow up and get with the program ... to fulfill his **'need'** for pleasure through some other more appropriate means. And even worse, she won't understand why that's a problem.

You see, while the estrogen is still flowing freely, women endure our alleged need for sexual pleasure much more willingly because they, too, share a measure of desire for physical intimacy. But when the estrogen in her system closes up shop and the rivers run dry, her desire drops to almost nothing, and she is not nearly as willing to put up with such nonsense anymore, especially considering how illegitimate this need appears to be.

When this happens, it's only natural for this **'luxury'** to fade away into almost nothingness because, based on **'the** perversion', it has no other purpose. As far as she is concerned, that was fun while it lasted, but we've got more important things to do now.

Oh nay nay ladies! Unfortunately, that's not the case. As already covered, **'the perversion'** is wrong. The idea that sex is an unnecessary luxury is a mentality that ignores the needs of the relationship. You may be able to get by without it just fine personally, but your marriage relationship cannot. And even at this age, your number one responsibility in life, behind God Himself, is still your relationship with your husband, and what that needs to thrive.

Along with that, it doesn't make any sense for the man to continue to be required to love his wife in her language after menopause if she is absolved of any responsibility to continue loving him in his. I don't know how anybody could see that as God's perfect design. Though there may have been a significant physiological change in her, the principles of agape remain the same.

I apologize if I sound like I am getting on you girls a little bit here. I don't mean it that way. We have all fallen prey to **'the perversion'** for so many years that we seem to accept it for the way we've always known it. You girls are not the problem. It's us, the church. We need to get back to the truth and teach it properly so that this type of damaging misconception stops happening.

I hope you can see what I am saying here. One of the most dangerous things about **'the perversion'** is that you never really see the kind of weakness it instills in your relationship until a challenging circumstance shows up. Then, when you need pure love and united support, you usually end up with some watered-down version of teamwork that leaves you with more questions and trust issues than it does a resolute faith in your spouse.

It's the same effect as putting Gallium on the surface of an Aluminum padlock, even though the lock body will retain its overall shape. After a while, the Gallium will have fused itself with the Aluminum and weakened it to a point where you can break the lock apart with your hands.

The Gallium works on the lock just like **'the perversion'** works on a marriage. It weakens the bond between the Aluminum molecules in the body of the lock. Then, when it is subjected to adverse pressure, instead of holding like it should, it just falls apart. Although the lock appeared sturdy, its core composition was compromised.

Menopause is just the kind of adverse pressure that can destroy a perversion-weakened marriage. This is because, as we clarified earlier, the language you girls speak allows you to function whether physical activity is present or not. Sexuality is only one of several things that ministers love and provide security to you, so if that drops off the list, you'll be able to adjust and keep moving without your whole world falling apart. The other things on the list help make up for what is missing.

We guys don't work that way, though. Our list has pretty much one thing on it: physical affirmation. Of course, there are many other things about you that are special and meaningful to us, but nothing ministers to us and gives us confidence in the relationship like your body can. When the flow of physical affirmation stops, we stop feeling loved.

If or when that happens, he most often retaliates by ceasing to do the things that make her feel loved.

I'm sure you can see where this is going. They are going to end up having more strife than peace, more fighting than loving. Essentially, they will discover that they no longer love each other. They are just not compatible.

Admittedly, this would seem like a logical explanation, but I believe that after all the living and working they've done together, they do still love each other, and probably very much. Somebody needs to help them get their focus back on the relationship instead of individual priorities. They have fallen prey to **'the perversion'** and now, with the effects of menopause added to the mix, are experiencing just how destructive it can be.

I believe the devil has propagated this lie for the sole purpose of keeping marriages weak enough for him to destroy whenever he feels like it. And since it is locked into our minds, into how we view a thing, it will stay there exactly the way it is for as long as we let it, until conscious efforts are made to change it.

On the flip side, think about this. How detrimental would the impact of menopause be if both he and she were already living by the understanding that their focus should be on keeping their relationship strong? And what if, because of this understanding, they were already proficient at loving each other selflessly in each other's own language?

Would adjustments still need to be made when menopause hits? Absolutely! But would the flow of love and passion get tripped up, fall apart, and grind to a complete stop? Absolutely NOT!

Loving your spouse and ministering to their need, whether you feel like it or not, is a big part of what this marriage agape is all about. As we've already established, focusing on and feeding your relationship helps you tackle the challenges life throws at your marriage while strengthening the bond between you at the same time. Then, even when menopause does show up, you can handle it because you're both functioning in selfless understanding, selfless love.

Now, there are certain drugs and medical things that can help deal with menopausal problems, and thank God for them, but ultimately, it comes down to whether or not we are willing to love this way. Are we humble enough to let go of those longstanding beliefs that are now comfortable to us and change? Are we willing to reprogram, to infuse our marriages with the kind of strength it takes to stay together, till death do us part?

This issue hit me several years ago when I was told of a longstanding friend who, with his wife of many years, loved God and served faithfully together in the church and ministry. I believe they were in their early 60s at the time. The next thing I know is they're divorced, and he was married to someone else, and rather quickly, too.

When asked about what happened, he very candidly explained that she didn't want to give him sex anymore, so he found someone who would and married her.

On one hand, I cannot agree with him leaving his wife to find a better sex partner. On the other hand, though, whether you are male or female, you cannot cut off the love that meets your spouse's needs and expect things to be OK. To do this would be asking for disaster to strike your marriage.

Now I'm not saying menopause caused my friends to break up. But I do think it is very believable that the effects of menopause, coupled with **'the perversion,'** could very well have been the source of their most significant disagreement. It sure looks like it anyway.

Ultimately, God has had a plan in place for us to handle whatever challenges our marriages may face, and it has been there since the beginning. It is agape. Therefore, the sooner we start developing ourselves in this design of selfless love for each other, the better prepared we will be when challenges like menopause present themselves. Then I can assure you, we will not be discovering that we don't love each other anymore.

♥ The Rights and Wrongs ♥

In this section, I'd like to add a little perspective to several different sexual **'options'** that exist in modern marriages. I'm sure many of you have either thought about or wondered whether it's OK for things like masturbation, anal sex, oral sex, bondage, toys, and all the other creative ways we humans have attempted to enhance our sexual experiences.

The most important consideration when thinking of such things is this. Why are you doing it, or considering it as an option?

This question requires an honest, gut-level assessment of your motives. The true answer to this is the key to determining whether or not you should participate in said behaviors.

Ultimately, the Bible tells us that the marriage bed is undefiled. This indicates that if both parties of a marriage are in agreement, whatever they do with each other is undefiled before God. This, however, is not the whole story.

At the beginning of this chapter, I reviewed some of the principles discussed in this book. I did this because all the nuggets in the chapter still align with and support the overall principles stated. Scripture is just like that. Even when you find those little nuggets of truth that deal with your specific curiosity, they are still going to flow with and through the larger principles that have been established.

Therefore, a better way to approach this kind of query is to say it like this. Within the guidelines laid out by the Word of God and the Spirit of Wisdom, the marriage bed is undefiled. Meaning, as long as you're in agreement with each other and not defiling any of the principles of truth, love, or wisdom laid out in scripture, you can do whatever you want.

An undeniable example of this would be having a three-some. It is easy to see that even if both people in the marriage claim they're okay with it, it still contradicts what the Word of God teaches us about love and marriage. Going that direction may stir up a particular kind of thrill in your sex life, but make no mistake, it will not make your marriage stronger. Those kinds of stirrings makes it weaker because it only feeds the sensual desires of the flesh. That passion is not pure, and the end result of it is a reprobate mind, which coincidentally has a way of making outright sin feel like something of great value to be desired. In other words, this should easily be a hard pass.

It is, however, just one small part of a larger conversation that is a somewhat dark area in marriage. This is probably because comparatively, very little is spoken about all the individual little sexual behaviors people wonder about. In many of these cases, the answers lie in some of the more general truths brought to us in scripture, which is why the attitude of your heart is so pivotal. It's why answering why you would be doing it has so much to do with whether or not you should go down that road.

It's also beneficial to do what Jesus said and *"count the cost."* (Luke 14:28). The benefit may be extra levels of excitement in your sex life, which in some cases may be what is needed, but what kind of potential dangers would each activity you are considering expose you to? You are both human beings and therefore have the exact nature as every other human. This means you could be opening the door to various physical and/or emotional challenges simply due to the weaknesses of your flesh. An objective and honest assessment of your own selves is beneficial in this. It's also beneficial to know how to follow the peace in your heart. Either way, determining whether or not the benefits outweigh the threats is significant.

I see it kind of like this. True undefiled sex is the act of intercourse between a man and the woman he is legally married to. All of these other activities under consideration are forms of foreplay intended to build up and prepare them for this act of becoming one (restoring wholeness.) With that in mind, there are a few things a person can consider when deciding what forms of this foreplay they are OK with.

Right away, it's easy to determine that any activity that takes your attention off of your spouse and places it on somebody else is an obvious boot. Some of the things in this category would be that threesome just mentioned, or wife-swapping, porn and being a swinger.

Then there are those activities that go against the way things are naturally made. Romans 1 uses the phrase, *"leaving the natural use of a woman."* Aside from what this particular section of scripture discusses, I believe it also serves as a guide for helping us understand how to approach certain activities. In other words, our bodies and their parts all have a designed function. When we go against the natural design and use, we are opening the door to more severe problems in the future. Anal sex would be one of the things in this category.

I'll explain. On a woman's body, there are only three openings large enough for a man to insert himself into. One of those openings, her anus, is very specifically made to be an exit (a simple conversation with an objective medical professional can clarify how very true this is). Well if you start regularly using this exit as an entrance you are going to expose yourselves to a myriad of potential challenges in your physical future.

Interestingly though, when sexual activity is involved, people tend to lose all sense of reality in order to accommodate their drives and desires. I had a neighbor across the alley from my wife's and my first house. He would earn money from welding projects in his shed out behind his house. For many years, he welded a wide range of items for people, helping to support his family through his efforts. Unfortunately, his welding ultimately led to his death because he wasn't ventilating his shed properly. Now in every one of your minds you are probably thinking he should have never been welding like that without proper ventilation. But he thought that it didn't matter because year after year he would go in and weld and it had no apparent effect on him. The truth is, one of the natural uses of a welder is proper ventilation. If you go against that natural use you may survive at first and appear to be just fine but at some point it will catch up to you and possibly even kill you.

In this example, it's easy for all of us to agree that nobody should ever weld without proper ventilation. Although we all know that a person can survive for a time or two, it is still a dangerous practice due to the potential consequences it could cause in the future. Therefore, it should be avoided. Well, it's easy for us all to agree with this idea when dealing with welding, but are you just as committed to this same principle when it's dealing with something sexual?

When you apply it to the world of sexuality, you can see that some activities are better to be avoided, not because they will send you straight to hell, but because of what they could cause in the future. The added challenges you may be exposing your physical and emotional self to may or may not show up right away, as with my neighbor's welding, but that doesn't mean it's a good or OK thing to do. This is where you and your spouse need to count the cost, as mentioned earlier. Consider the potential and determine just what kind of value it would bring to your pursuit of restoring wholeness, and whether or not that makes it worth it. Essentially, you need to decide whether the potential benefits are sufficient to outweigh the possible issues that could arise.

The Bible may not have a specific verse addressing the one thing you are wondering about, but sometimes taking a more practical approach helps us identify where the steps of wisdom are. Scripture talks a lot about wisdom, identifying it as *"the principle thing"* (Proverbs 4:7). So any time you can align yourself with it, you know you can have confidence in what you're doing.

Now, I consider any activity not covered by these first two to be part of one big miscellaneous category that is more like a free-for-all. Among them are things like masturbation, oral sex, toys, lotions, bondage, voyeurism, role playing, etc... Each of these though can be addressed in much the same manner so this next part will cover all of it.

SIDE NOTE: The agreement you have with your spouse is the filter that determines what things make it through to experiential mode. This makes it very important for you to let the filter do its job. If you keep pushing on it and pushing on it, you could mess it up, and then all kinds of contaminants could make it through into your marriage.

As it is stated at the beginning of this section, the motive of your heart is the key. Why are you doing this thing? Why are you considering doing this thing?

To identify where your own personal heart is you need to know the difference between the sensual desires of your flesh person and the passionate drive that draws you closer together. Ask yourself some simple questions:

> ➤ Does this activity make me want my spouse more or just more of the activity?
> ➤ Will this activity fulfill my spouse as much as it does me?
> ➤ Could I do this if I became keenly aware that Holy Spirit was watching me?

These questions, or others very similar to them, compel you to confront yourself, your marriage relationship, and your inner spirit. If they don't all agree, then there may be a problem before it even starts. You probably want to let it go, or at the least, just ponder those things in your heart for a little while and then revisit them at a later time.

If they all do agree then you know which direction to go. If they say no, it's a boot. If they all say yes, then you can send it to the filter. Talk about it with your spouse. Give them a chance to express their heart on it, and then come to an agreement. Then, if that's all a yes. check your peace. If you have peace about it, you are in agreement with each other and agreement with yourself then go for it. The marriage bed is undefiled.

The fact is, even though these questions can be answered with a simple yes or no, they are not straightforward yes-or-no questions. The only way to get an accurate yes or no is to dive into your heart and identify what you are after. Simply put, it's normal to have different sexual desires. It's also normal to want to experience them. But when fulfilling your personal sexual desires becomes more important than fulfilling what the relationship requires, you are not being motivated by the right spirit.

In that, the Bible is very clear, even if you are doing wrong. Father is not going to judge you, turn His back on you, or burn you to a crisp with holy fire from Heaven. Instead, He will be the poster child for what the fruits of the Spirit are supposed to look like in everyday life with you. However, you need to know that, just like my neighbor with his welding, an accepting response from Father does not mean you got away with it or that it was even OK. In those same verses that tell us we are free from all this judgment and shame, it also tells us that the things we so choose will become our gods. And in this arena of sexual desire this is very important to know because even though you are married you can still very much be serving the god of sexual pleasure. You can get away with it for a while but it will eventually catch up with you, and maybe even kill you.

That might sound a little harsh, but don't be dismayed. I am not suggesting that you can't do anything fun or creative in your love life. I am, however, wanting to make sure that you understand that whatever activities you and your spouse are doing, you're doing them in the right spirit, that it's undefiled. So much so that unless it's an activity that directly offends the truth and wisdom of the Bible, you don't need to get too caught up worrying about what is right or wrong. Instead, get caught up with identifying where your hearts are and where they are going.

If you're looking at it because you're both sincerely motivated to do what you can to invigorate the passion between you, then go for it. Try it out a couple of times. Check your spirits and be honest with each other. Do you feel OK, or do you have lingering reservations? I like to say, do you feel like you have a red light or a green light? If either one or both of you gets a red light, then there's your answer. Don't go there any more. If you both have this green-light sense of peace, then go ahead and enjoy it.

Now, if you are secretly satisfying some long-time fantasy or trying to keep yourself happy, then you need to check your motives. Your spouse is not a special toy given to you to fulfill your fantasies and desires with. They are there to be one with you. Therefore, in this situation, it wouldn't matter what the activity was. It would not be OK because the heart's not right.

There will be seasons where you are both much more free with your sexual expression towards each other, and then there will be those times when you are much more reserved. There may be times when you engage in certain things that are not a part of what is typical, simply for the sake of making it through a tough time. Or maybe because of injury or the process of healing, one would like to but can't perform the way they usually would, so they need a little help. Sometimes you are separated for longer times than you can handle. Stuff happens. The point is, your sexuality is a part of your relationship, so it will breathe and move along with everything else going on between the two of you. And like with everything else, if your hearts are true, somehow or another, you will always find your way back to peace.

Keep in mind that, like with anything, sometimes your mind isn't yet sure how to handle new or different things in your life. This is not the test though. It's all about your heart and whether there is peace.

So here it is. Within the confines of marriage, there is a special place where freedom abides. It's a freedom to learn and grow, to try new things and solidify proven things. Some of those things will work and some won't but there is no shame in your efforts to grow closer together. It's all about becoming increasingly one. Your sexuality will grow in the same way all the other things in your relationship grow. A lot of it comes through trial and error, so don't be afraid. Be honest enough to say no when it doesn't feel right and brave enough to try new things when it feels necessary.

Remember that *"all things work together for good to those who love God..."* (Romans 8:28). This means: as long as you keep your hearts in the right place, even if you do start doing things you really shouldn't be doing, your hearts will lead you back. God will protect and keep you as He guides you to peace.

Your heart is the key.

♥ The Total Package ♥

Well now. That sounds interesting.

For the sake of discussion, please humor me and consider that a marriage consists of two main offices, the office of husband and the office of wife. Each one is equal in authority, equal in value, and equal in necessity to the marriage's ability to function correctly. The people who fill these offices were designed and built to function in those capacities.

So then, what exactly do these offices do? Well, generally speaking, men conquer, and women nurture. If it were possible to hook an analyzer up to the heart of a male test subject and set it to read **"Modus Operandi"**, in almost every instance, it would read, **"Conquer."**

The very way men are physically built testifies to this. They have almost twice as many red blood cells as women do, increased density in their muscle tissue, usually larger in size and have more stamina to boot.

Psychologically, men are designed to utilize those physical characteristics fully. They are typically all go-go-go from beginning to end. Nothing less than accomplishment will do, so let's get after it. Don't stop till it's done. It all screams, **"Built to conquer!"**

On top of that, figure in those factory-installed motivations which are driven to provide, protect and lead his family. In computer terms, these are like the firmware drivers that run his hardware. These functions are so ingrained into how he sees himself, they're like instincts.

This means that in a man's drive for wholeness, obtaining his woman is only the start. From then on, he is driven to accomplish and conquer these three fundamental duties of man. This knowledge is essential because if he is not able to complete this mission, this destined duty, he will not feel like much of a man. His psyche will tell him his performance is unacceptable, and therefore, he is intolerable.

It sounds a bit brutal, I know, but that's kind of about what it is.

On the ladies' side of things, if you could take that same analyzer and hook it up to her heart, in almost every instance it would read, **"Nurture."**

Just as with men, women are built to nurture, from their physical composition to their psychological make-up to the motivations in their hearts. It is just as instinctual for a woman to care for and restore her home (which includes her family) as it is for a man to conquer the role of providing, protecting, and leading. And also just like the men, this is so ingrained in her that when a woman is not able to do it she does not feel like much of a woman.

In everyday life, when a man is trying to do things for his wife that he believes is protecting, providing or leading and she shuts him down because she doesn't feel like it's necessary, she's not letting him be a man. From her perspective, it is most likely just a harmless assessment of legitimate need. But when you filter it through his psychological structure this is very much a restriction of his manhood. She is not letting him do what he was created to do for her.

On the flip side, when a woman is doing things for her husband that deal with his well-being, both in and out of their home, he will typically try to shut her down because he thinks she's treating him like a child. In fact, he's not letting her be a woman. From his perspective, it is most likely a harmless response to what appears to be over-obsessing about something unnecessary. But when you filter it through her psychological make-up this is very much a restriction of her womanhood. He is not letting her do what she was created to do for him.

You see, just as God is a package deal, men and women are also package deals. They are the epitome of that age-old idea of, **"You can't have one without the other."** In other words, as much as you may know God as being good and loving, you cannot ignore the fact that He is also just and holy. You don't get one side of the pendulum without the other. In order to truly understand who He is, you must accept all of who He is.

It's the same thing with us. If you are a husband and want your wife to be your passionate lover and faithful supporter, then you will need to be willing to listen and talk a lot. She's going to want to know how your day is going and that you are alright. She'll fuss about your wrinkled shirt and want to make sure you've brushed your teeth. This is because when a woman's heart opens up to love you, she will naturally try to nurture you. It's her mission. You don't get one side without the other.

As a wife, if you want your husband to be gentle and understanding but also your fierce and gallant knight in shining armor, you're going to need to be willing to follow when he leads you and listen when he bluntly tells you as he sees it. What you might interpret as rudeness may very well be him trying to protect you from the dragons. What you might consider stubborn and insensitive may very well be him caring for you enough to tell you what you need, rather than what you want. This is because when a man's heart opens up to love you he will naturally set out to conquer you, which in his heart means to provide for you, protect you and lead you into your future. It's his mission. You don't get one side without the other.

This is an important consideration because of Genesis 2:25. Once again it identifies for us that when you are married, you have a responsibility to create a relational atmosphere your spouse can feel free to be vulnerable or open in. And though your feelings are not what you would build on or guide your lives by, they are a definite indicator of the health of your relationship. The reason this is so important to understand is that there is nothing more frustrating, more restrictive to a man's heart than when his woman doesn't let him be the man he was wired to be. There is likewise nothing more frustrating or binding to a woman's heart than when her husband doesn't let her be the woman she was wired to be.

Listen. If you are a wife, you need to let your conqueror conquer, even if it's inconvenient for you. If you are a husband, you need let your nurturer nurture, even if it's inconvenient for you. It's not always easy but it is an integral part of learning how to love selflessly. It's growing in agape.

Please allow me to put it this way. Men, you have a choice. You can choose to keep accusing her of nagging you and treating you like a child, or you can acknowledge that the care that drives her to treat you that way is also the exact same care that motivates her to present herself to you in the bedroom.

It's the same with women. You also have a choice. You can continue accusing him of being rude, stubborn and insensitive, or you can acknowledge that the motivation causing him to be that way is also the very same thing that makes him willing to sit with you and listen to what you are saying and hold you when you're troubled, etc.

These kinds of expressions are so natural to the individuals that many times they don't even realize they're doing it. Even if their spouse feels more annoyed by it than loved, make no mistake. It is most assuredly the very same love as the kind that produces the responses you desire. It's just manifesting from the other side of the same coin.

With that being said, I think you have probably already picked up on how important it is for married people to exercise self-control. It is not OK to flippantly say whatever you feel like saying, or do whatever you feel like doing under the guise of,

"It's just the way I am."

Without self control, these natural expressions of love become more about making sure your own self is covered than it is about genuinely caring for the other person. Self control will identify the line where that which is truly natural stops, and then it will go no further.

In other words, we need to pay very close attention to how we say and do the things that are natural expressions of our hearts. Because men and women are wired so differently, it is way too easy for your simple act of care to be completely misunderstood. And believe me when I say, these kinds of misunderstandings can cause a lot of hurtful responses. It is just like the old saying goes, **"It's not what you're saying. It's how you're saying it."** or, **"It's not what you're doing. It's how you're doing it."**

The idea is this. Just because the things you are saying and doing are natural expressions of who you are doesn't mean you can say and do those things without any tempering. It's OK to say the things you say and do the things you do, but every bit of it needs to be filtered through 1 Corinthians 13 before it's ever seen or heard by your spouse.

Through my experience over the years, in ninety-nine times out of a hundred, whenever someone uses the phrase, **"It's just the way I am."** it is just an excuse for a lack of self-control. And in those cases, the behaviors being defended usually don't resemble the way God wants us to be.

I'm going to be blunt here. There is no Bible verse, zero-nada-none that justify behavior that is the product of a lack of self control. Jesus did not lose control of Himself when He turned over the tables and kicked the money changers out of the temple. He didn't lose control of His tongue when He insulted the religious leaders and pretty much put them in their place. Neither He nor any other verse in Scripture is justification for you losing your temper or letting your lips flap in the breeze because you're upset, angry, fed-up or even overwhelmed by somebody else.

Look. Experiencing all of those emotions don't make us bad people. One reason God gave us His Spirit is because He knew we would face these things. Our goal is to keep our cool enough to stay respectful and caring, even when we are upset. With His help we can temper ourselves so when we get overwhelmed, we can process those feelings in a way that doesn't hurt or alienate other people, especially those closest to us.

So arm yourself with this knowledge. Consider it a weapon against strife and division. By giving your spouse the freedom to be who and what they are, you are creating an environment that helps them feel like they are able to do what they were created to do. Remember. Their programming came from the factory, meaning God designed them that way. When you fight against it you are attacking who they are as a person. You could say you're attacking their manhood/womanhood.

That verse in Genesis 2 refers to the two of you being able to be naked together and feel no shame. The way this subject plays out has a significant impact on whether or not you can experience what this verse is talking about.

As you grow and mature, you most definitely get better at working together and relating to each other. Through improving how you express yourselves and intentionally understanding each other, you learn how your relationship can be a source of peace and appreciation. You end up with a relationship that **'conquers'** every challenge and **'nurtures'** your heart. After all, they're both the equivalent expression from opposite sides of the same coin. They are the total package.

♥ *Finally... Forgiveness* ♥

How could I write a whole chapter filled with nuggets of truth for your marriage and not talk about forgiveness? Sorry. I can't.

Forgiveness is on the list of things your marriage relationship cannot survive without, like thankfulness, perseverance, and ice cream (Hmmm).

This need is so elementary and obvious that it almost seems like a waste of time and space to even discuss it. That is why I want to leave the basics of forgiveness in your hands. Most likely, you already understand that when your spouse messes up, you need to forgive them. If you don't, it can grow into a much deeper offense and even bitterness. This condition can turn your heart and desire against your spouse. It will also make life quite a bit more difficult for them as they work around and through the dark cloud you keep holding over their head.

Relationally, unforgiveness is the equivalent of using your kitchen drain to get rid of cooking grease. Sure, you can get away with it the first time, and the second, third or however many times after that. However, eventually, you will have a serious and potentially expensive clog on your hands. Unforgiveness starts building up and accumulating until your relationship stops growing altogether. When that happens, all that yucky crud you've been discreetly trying to get rid of gets blown back up in your face for all the world to see.

Ultimately, offenses that are not forgiven can damage or even destroy your marriage. That's pretty much it in a nutshell.

As you refresh that reality in your hearts, I would still like to share a couple of things that I see about forgiveness. The first will deal with protecting yourself from subtle offenses. Then we'll look at one of the most potent things forgiveness can do for you. As we proceed, I'd like to clarify that I am focusing solely on the effects of forgiveness and unforgiveness on the marriage relationship. These principles will apply to any relationship in your life, though I am speaking specifically about marriages in this section.

Starting off, for the sake of the discussion, I have loosely organized everything needing forgiveness into two categories, obvious and subtle. By obvious, I mean the offenses you see in front of you, staring right back in your face every time you look inside your heart. You can't miss these guys. They make it pretty apparent that you've got something needing your attention.

The amount of stress and trouble you experience from these offenses is directly proportional to the amount of time it takes you to deal with them appropriately.

The other category is the ones that are more subtle. These are the offenses that either get brushed off or intentionally tucked deep inside, out of the way so as not to interfere with this life you're trying to live. These guys are like a bottle of deadly poison that gets buried in the backyard. Very soon, you forget it's there, so you live as if it doesn't exist. As the bottle deteriorates, the poison leaks out and starts killing everything from the ground up. Randomly, one day you discover your yard is dying, and you can't figure out why.

PRINCIPLE ALERT:

One of the main ways the devil deceives people is by convincing them they are doing just fine, even though they may be setting themselves up for difficulty or failure. This concept is a take-off of the original temptation he threw at Eve in the Garden. God told them that if they ate that certain fruit they would die. When the devil got her to eat the fruit, surprisingly she didn't drop over dead. This would have caused her to think that maybe the snake knew what it was talking about. Because she apparently 'got away with it', she was given the impression that she was just fine.

In looking back, though she was still alive I don't think any of you would agree that she was **'just fine'** after that. Though the natural world did not respond quite like anyone would have expected, that didn't mean they **'got away with it.'** We can easily see that from that moment on, Adam and Eve were living on borrowed time.

I would caution you. Don't be deceived. God is not mocked. Whatever He has said, you can pretty much take to the bank. No matter how **'just fine'** you may feel while doing your own thing, His word will still be accomplished. In other words, the experiences in your life may be telling you that God's word and design do not work for or apply to you, but they do. In the end, the actual truth of it will be seen. Isaiah 55:11 makes this pretty clear... *"So shall My word* *be that goes forth from My mouth; It shall not return to Me void, but it shall accomplish what I please, and it shall prosper in the thing for which I sent it."*

The point in this principle is this. Just because you don't see, hear, or feel any of the natural results you think you should see in response to your certain behaviors, do not think it's over and done with. Your senses can only tell you how you are feeling in the present. God's word covers your present and your future. Feeling perfectly alright with yourself today does not mean you will be OK tomorrow. This is especially true if your actions today lead you away from God's leading and protection. What you do today sets you up for tomorrow.

God has given us His Word so that we would know the blueprint for a healthy and prosperous life. The devil works hard to convince people they can live by their own design and still be just as healthy and prosperous. A lot of people fall for it, too, because the long-term effects of this mentality are generally imperceptible in the heat of the moment. This causes them to think they are just fine when in fact, they are walking into imminent pain and suffering... the very thing God was trying to protect them from.

With Adam and Eve, when they ate that fruit, the process of dying started in them. They did not know their physical death was now imminent because it was imperceptible to their natural senses at that moment. And most likely, when some of the negative fruits of their decision started showing up in other parts of their lives, they still didn't get it. Without divine revelation they would not have been able to make that correlation.

So once again, do not be deceived. Trust the Word of God over the things you see and feel in the natural world. It'll help you attain what you are believing God for. Even more, it will prevent the devil from influencing your will through **'the deception of natural perception'**. It is no coincidence that the Bible tells us four times in four different places, *"The just shall live by faith."* (Habakuk 2:4, Romans 1:17, Galatians 3:11, and Hebrews 10:38).

Because of this I wanted to point out that the most dangerous forms of unforgiveness are the ones you don't see. These are the ones that are stewing and brewing down in your heart, but you don't realize it because, in the moment, they are imperceptible to the naked eye. They have either been ignored or emotionally tucked away, thus making you feel like you are just fine.

As time goes by, you may even begin to experience some of the fruits of this unforgiveness in other parts of your life, but without divine revelation, you would not be able to make that correlation.

The obvious idea here is to prevent any offense from drifting out of sight, out of mind. In so doing, this one little rule will serve you well. **Every offense gets a decision.** It doesn't matter how big or small it is. When something happens, you need to make a conscious decision about it. You are not allowed to treat it like it didn't happened. You are not allowed to avoid it or brush past it. You must choose something.

Now it's true that some offenses may take a little more time to work through than others, but the decision still needs to be made. That's what sets the direction for the ship. It identifies the goal and demonstrates your heart. Pointing out your purpose also gives your faith something to work toward. It all starts with a decision.

Deuteronomy 30:19 is not just a one-shot wonder for your life. It is supposed to be a daily function, and protecting relationships is a big reason why... *"I call Heaven and earth as witnesses today against you, that I have set before you life and death, blessing and cursing; therefore choose life, that both you and your descendants may live;"*

The truth is, even if you don't choose forgiveness, it is still of vital importance that you make a decision. At the very least, you will face the issue and take action to prevent it from becoming imperceptible. In so doing, you are making it obvious and acknowledging that something needs your attention. It's a roundabout way, but a way nonetheless of taking the first steps toward resolution.

Now, I would like to encourage you a bit, if I may. I'm sure most of you already understand that unforgiveness is a product of pride. It usually doesn't come out of arrogant pride, those pompous attitudes we generally associate with prideful people. It typically stems from the kind of pride that trusts your own senses over the wisdom spoken by God and others who love you. It is rooted in fear and self-preservation. Understandably, this pride struggles to let things go.

If this is you, take heart. You are not broken or bad. It's pretty normal to be this way. You see, your nature is set to allow you to function in this natural world, whether or not you ever allow Jesus to be your Lord. This means that a lot of the things you do naturally are things that are relative to the ways of this natural world. Because you abide in this physical world, the natural way you function is appropriate, or normal. It is your programmed way of being.

The difficulty you inevitably run into is that since Adam's sin, your nature is flawed. It is very much geared toward making you safe and happy right now, and only in a natural way. It will even do this at the expense of your future. This programming ends up creating all sorts of side-effect issues that make your life even more complicated, even though you're just trying to correct one thing. It's almost exactly like the multiple disclaimers you hear in commercials for the latest and greatest medication. You may be effectively getting rid of your foot fungus, but the side effects of that medication could give you a heart attack, stroke, insomnia, headaches, joint pain, constipation, or in some cases, death.

The beauty of the Gospel is how Jesus came and provided a way for you to live beyond the limitations of this natural realm and your natural human nature. You still need this nature while living in this world, be its flaws no longer hinder you. This essentially means that when you are faced with an offence, you are choosing between your spirit nature and your natural nature? In choosing forgiveness or unforgiveness, you are choosing life or death, blessing or cursing.

As a married person who has a spouse who needs you, *"Thus says the Lord of hosts: Consider your ways!"* (Haggai 1:7). Who are you going to trust, your feelings or God? Of course, I'm going to tell you not to trust your feelings, because your feelings will lie, and without any regret. If you don't believe me, ask an anorexic if she/he feels skinny. Their feelings have lied to them so hard that we had to give it a name and a condition. You see, truth and lie do not exist in the world of pure emotion, so your feelings can tell you anything. Do you trust that?

Then there is God. God is deeply invested in your wholeness. He cares about you being able to live the good life He planned for you. Because of this, He is very committed to give you **the truth, the whole truth, and nothing but the truth.** He wants you to be prepared and equipped for success throughout your entire life. Part of His equipping involves keeping you free from emotional clutter... forgiveness.

For everything that happens in your relationship, no matter how great or small, a decision is necessary. So choose, and choose life... It'll be OK. Go ahead and shut the door to imperceptible unforgiveness.

Lastly, I would like to reference some benefits of forgiveness. After all, if it is of such importance to your marriage, then the pitfalls of unforgiveness cannot be the only thing it presents. There must be something it does that is so beneficial, you don't want to live without it. So let's take a look.

This will also tap into the conversation contrasting the natural part of you and the spiritual part. You see, the pains of offense are wounds to your soul. Your spirit is not damaged by what happens to you emotionally, but it can most definitely be limited, or hindered by the condition of your soul.

This is significant because your nature and your soul work very closely together. When your soul perceives something good, something bad, something helpful, something dangerous, etc., your nature triggers your mind, will, and emotions to respond. These natural responses are something the devil has spent considerable time studying over the centuries. Because he is so familiar with it, he has become very adept at manipulating people to respond in ways that will ultimately set them up for failure. To them, it is generally imperceptible. Without divine revelation they would not be able to make that correlation.

The devil can't beat your spirit. But if he can render your spirit inoperable by binding up your soul, he gets a win. When you wade through all the froth and bubble, the gritty details expose the devil's primary deception... his greatest weakness. The only way he can get to you is through your soul.

Do you remember Ephesians 6:12? *"For we do not wrestle against flesh and blood, but against principalities, against powers, against the rulers of the darkness of this age, against spiritual hosts of wickedness in heavenly places."*

The enemy of your soul is not that person who keeps hurting your feelings. The misunderstandings and offenses that keep happening are the product of those spirits of darkness taking advantage of your natural patterns of response. They will use them and use them until it either ruins you or stops working. This demonic operation has one primary purpose: take out your spirit by binding up your soul. And this, people, is why forgiveness is so powerful.

Forgiveness wipes out all the effects of hurtful offenses in your soul. It sets you free from the weight that tries to encumber you with feelings of being victimized. It delivers you from the stress and emotional pain that was inflicted. Essentially, it destroys the most effective strategy the enemy has against you.

With the sting of offense removed, the bulk of the devil's ability to derail your spirit is effectively neutralized. Forgiveness is an infinite-use trump card God has given you to protect your soul from harm. If you don't bite the baited hook, you'll never get caught. It is all about protecting and delivering your own self, the one who was offended, instead of sheepishly letting the guilty party go free without your justified judgment. Choosing to forgive will set your soul free, with no regrets.

So, why then? If forgiveness is so great, why is unforgiveness still such a problem?

Consider this. When your soul has been injured, your nature responds to that danger by drawing you into yourself. Your first instinct is to protect yourself from more danger, then pursue a safe path out to a safe place. This is as natural a human response as there is. To whatever degree, and for whatever amount of time it takes, the focus goes inward. The greater the perceived threat, the more pressing these needs become. Also, be careful because this type of response system can cause a herbivore to bite like a carnivore. I'm sure you have already seen how this fight-or-flight response mechanism is not limited to physical threats. It is employed just as proficiently for those intangible threats to the soul as well. Whether physical or emotional, they feel just as real.

Now, as real as they are, the offenses you deal with in marriage are hopefully not the kind of threat that will physically kill you. So, every time you deal with one, you are put in a position to consider what you value most. Feeling the need to protect yourself is a normal human response. But forgiveness sets your soul free from the damaging effects of offense. Are you going to trust your senses? Or are you going to trust God? Do you value the feelings of security you get from taking matters into your own hands? Or do you value the peace and joy and confidence you get from trusting Him to take care of you? Most of us would say we value both, but what do you value more?

You see, the side effects of choosing to trust yourself are things like restlessness, anxiety and strife, confusion and every evil work having its way in your home. And to make matters worse, there isn't a whole lot Holy Spirit can do about it because your will has chosen its course. But, if your will chooses to trust Him by facing the offense, forgiving and letting it go, suddenly there is a lot He can do. As powerful and almighty as God is, it still takes the decision of your will to open the door and release His power to do what it does. You must be willing to let the pain go into His care. You must be willing to choose life.

When considering these truths, you begin to see that it's your will, not God's omnipotent power, that determines what will happen next. Let that resonate in you for a minute. God has designed things in such a way that in your life, your will has the authority to release or restrict His power. Choosing to do your own thing your own way is a choice to shut Him down, and He will honor your will. He will not force you to be submissive to His desire for you. But choosing to follow His recommended way of living releases His power to work in and through you. So again, what you choose is paramount in determining your future.

With that, trust me when I say that there is no judgment towards people who struggle with forgiveness. Choosing against your own nature is not easy, especially if the offenses against you were egregious. But fear not. There is always hope in Christ. I've met a lot of people who have been through some horrible things in their lives. Yet today, because of their choices, they have peace and joy in their hearts. So much so that unless they decide to tell you about their experiences, you would never know something had happened. Since God is not a respecter of persons, you too can expect that same peace and love and harmony forgiveness will bring, if you so choose. You are not so hopelessly locked into your humanity that the power of God can't help you, *"Because with natural man these things may feel impossible, but they are not impossible with God. For with God, all these things are possible."* (Mark 10:27, paraphrased).

This blows the door wide open to another truth for you to consider. Forgiveness is just as much an act of faith as becoming a Christian is. And it's a good thing, too, because there will be times when your soul, in and of itself, does not have the ability to forgive. I have been there myself and have found that I can still make the right choice. By acknowledging the weakness in my own flesh, I can still choose to forgive... by faith. I may not feel like it, but by God, I'm going to do it. Once I've established my decision, every time the memory of that offense pops back up, I repeat myself all over again as if it was yesterday. Yes, I may still feel hurt and broken by what happened. Yes, I may still be struggling to think proper thoughts about that person. Yes, my flesh is still weak, but in Jesus' name, I choose forgiveness! Choosing to trust God and submit to Him helps me because, even though I may not be able to see or feel it, my faith assures me that my forgiveness is real. This gives me hope. It proves 1John 5:4... *"For whatever is born of God overcomes the natural ways of this natural world. And this is the victory that has overcome the natural ways of this natural world - our faith."* (paraphrased).

So there it is. Many times, forgiveness is nothing more than a simple act of faith. At other times, it is the result of being disciplined enough to make a decision about every offense. Either way, faith is involved. Either way, we know it is not beyond our reach. By faith, we can choose forgiveness; we can choose life every time. It is the way.

Through choosing forgiveness, the list of benefits that infiltrate your life extends beyond what your finite mind can process. The multiple levels of impact and domino-effect chains of events change and expand exponentially. They are beyond calculation. It is a massive benefit to avoid the snarling and strife that comes with unforgiveness. Then consider how valuable it is to be able to neutralize the devil's most effective strategy against your soul. These benefits produce their own benefits, such as being able to walk in confidence and enjoy the joy life brings. You also have to include the benefits of unity, which include peace and harmony with your spouse. And we absolutely must acknowledge the added spice forgiveness brings by bellowing up the flames of passion and desire for each other. The overall area of effect (AOE) of forgiveness reaches out to every part of your life and screams as loud as it can, **"Worth it! It may not be easy sometimes, but it is worth it!"**

In wrapping up my thoughts, let me review. We all know the side effects of harboring unchecked offense. It can and will poison your soul. Therefore, you do not want to allow any offense to present itself without making a decision about it. In doing so, it will not be able to slip from view and cause damage undetected. The last thing you want is to think you are doing just fine when you have a potentially dangerous issue to deal with.

Then, understand that forgiveness does an even greater work in you than it does in the person who hurt you. It liberates your soul from the devil's most effective strategy against you. It allows you to experience what it means to have true free will. This free will is essential because by God's design, it is your will, not His omnipotent power, that determines what will happen next.

So, what do you value most? I call Heaven and Earth as witness today that I have set before you life and death, blessing and cursing. So choose life. Let forgiveness be final.

♥ Closing Thoughts ♥

I believe it is safe to say we all have a desire for peace. Within marriage, this desire is even stronger. We have this natural inclination that conflict and relational challenges work against the perfect kind of love we envision while daydreaming about living that fairy tale version of happily ever after.

Interestingly enough, it seems like whenever I pray for peace in my marriage, God always gives me something to work on. I need to be more patient. I need to be more understanding or in better control of my temper. I need to walk in forgiveness. He never tells me what my wife needs to do for me to feel better. I'm sure the same is true for all of you too.

It is important to remember that no matter what challenge you are facing now or what you have been through before, relational physics is still going to function the same way for you as it does for everyone else. This is because, no matter how tough your life has been, you are still human. You still have the same basic programming as everyone else. So, whether or not your way of handling life has been altered by the difficulties you have endured, the principles of working together and growing into oneness remain the same. At some point everyone will have to follow the same relational guidelines if they want to live in peace and unity with each other.

For example, the Bible says *"A soft answer turns away wrath, but a harsh word stirs up anger."* (Proverbs 15:1). Now it doesn't matter where you've come from or how different you are from normal, if you respond to people with gentleness and care you will diffuse a lot of trouble before it starts. This is also true for the other half of the verse. If you respond to people with defensive or cold vocal tones using words that focus on content over care, you're going to be starting something, because humans are still humans.

I understand this may sound a bit ominous for some of you, but do not fret. This same reality is true of the Gospel as well. Anything the devil can do God can do better. It doesn't matter how complex your life has been or how different you have become. God has already prepared for your restoration.

In other words, if you set your determination to do the same things everyone else has to do to develop peace in their hearts, you will have it too. The power of God working in and through you is not affected in any way by your present condition or how you got there. His love does what it does despite you, and it never fails.

The decision for peace and harmony ultimately rests with you. How badly do you want it? Do you want it enough to change how you do life? You can be assured that if you choose yes, you will have to grow. For God to do His work in your relationship, He must do it in you first. But be assured. It absolutely can be done.

This means that no matter how self-focused you may be, how insecure or codependent you feel, or emotionally altered you've ended up being, you can be free. You can have peace. You can live in harmony. Choose to trust God and let Holy Spirit guide you. He will always lead you to a place of strength and wholeness. He will always lead you to a place where your marriage is strong.

Conclusion

*W*ell it looks like we're coming in for the landing so I need to wrap this up.

I'm sure you've noticed that I repeat myself a lot. I have probably said, **"feed and foster your passions"**, or **"feed your relationship"**, or **"foster your love for each other"**, or something along those lines several hundred times through the course of this book, more or less.

Even though you may have grown weary of hearing it, I wanted to repeat it enough times for it to be indelibly etched into your minds. When you think of anything about marriage, I want the words **'feed and foster your passions for each other'** to automatically pop into your head.

In other words, at the risk of becoming unbearably redundant, I want to help shape your thoughts about marriage to be on things that will have a profound and positive impact. By God's design, your marriage was made to last, so if there is any part I can play to help it do just that, I will at least try.

With that, let me remind you. God made us in our opposite ways to complement each other. These differences were never intended to be the most significant cause of dissidence and division between us. Instead, they were intended to provide us with the solid path to unity and be a source of passion.

Focusing on your relationship so it is your first consideration is crucial, especially within the body of Christ. Up to this point in our history, something has been missing in our attempts to defend and hold our marriages. Getting back to patterning our relationships with each other after our relationship with God is the place to start. After all, Jesus is our bridegroom.

In that, let's acknowledge and be thankful for the resources that have already been made available to us. Yes, I have referred to the silence of the Church several times in these pages, but there are exceptions. There are special people among us, wonderful Christian people who are willing to teach, write, and be a voice to the world about true sexuality. We need to support them as much as possible and take up the torch with them. It's time for the whole Body to wake up and be a Spirit-led voice of truth to our world... in every area of life.

If you are one of these teachers, Thank you! Thank you for being willing to be real with the Body of Christ. Thank you for your work and for the life you have given to carry this torch. Thank you for caring for our marriages.

For the rest of us, look. Conveying this type of wisdom feels really awkward, which is one reason we've avoided it like we have. But if Holy Spirit is opening a door, there must be a need. Which means, if He is not afraid to talk about it, then you don't need to be either. This generation needs a Godly, Spirit-led voice that is speaking truth, even in the area of sexuality. And don't worry. Even though this spirit and society seem more like an established Goliath, steadfast in its stand for the deception it believes, always remember. Goliath died... hard.

At the very least, we need to be willing to pass this understanding on to our children. As much as the spirit of the world would like to keep them ignorant, they deserve to know the truth. And they deserve it the way God has provided it for them. They need to know that marriage, and the essential elements that make marriage strong, are nothing to be ashamed of. Whether Christian or not, doing marriage the right way is a worthy challenge with irreplaceable value. And they need to hear it first, and foremost, from their mom and dad.

Look. This fairy tale idea that you can magically meet your true love and live happily ever after is, for the most part, exactly that, a fairy tale. Those of you who have been around a while know it. I mean, coming from opposite sides of the coin, coupled with growing up in different circumstances is challenging enough to work through when you get married. It is even more complicated if the two of you come from different nations or cultures. Then add to the mix how many of us are still learning how to just be a proper person, while learning the art of being an adequate spouse at the same time. Then when you sprinkle in all those lovely challenges life likes to throw at you, you can get overwhelmed rather quickly. Sometimes it's not easy. That whole concept of living happily ever after isn't like it's made out to be, but striving for it is still worth the effort.

Fortunately, when you get married, you get to learn and grow together. You're not doing it alone anymore. This means you are growing as a person alongside your spouse while growing together as a couple. Having the other half of you present and accounted for makes a huge difference, even though it will still challenge you up one side and down the other. It's all wildly fantastic and frustrating to the bone. At times it feels like the best thing you've ever done while other times it makes you wonder what on earth ever convinced you to do such a crazy thing.

Yet,through all the learning and growing together, the struggles and the triumphs, one thing remains true. God is the steadfast foundation of it all. And He is not shaken. He is not worried, and He is not upset with you when you mess up. He loves you passionately. He cares for you deeply. And He has already provided a way of restoration.

He is your trump card. As I've mentioned throughout this book, God is our ultimate source. Nothing here on earth will set your heart ablaze like the presence of God can.

Seeking Him and fostering your relationship with Him fills your heart with the ability to love like He loves… agape.

When your heart is in tune with Father's heart, passion becomes your driving force. You grow from simply maintaining your love to knowing how to stay **'in love'** with each other. Feeding your passionate desires will keep your hearts on fire. While those flames blaze through your souls they are purifying you and transforming you into the lover your spouse needs most. This passion is your love's source of ignition and has been since *"In the beginning."* (Genesis 1:1). And why not. It comes straight from the heart of God.

So with that in mind, here are a couple things to remember. Number one, **Yes! It is worth it!** Nobody who is legitimately doing marriage right ever wishes they were single again. Maybe there are times when they wish they weren't stuck with that idiot they married. But even in those times, they still work it out and end up growing closer together. This is because, at its lowest point, marriage still provides more for you than it could ever take away.

A good marriage is like the blessing of the Lord. *"It'll make you rich and ultimately add no sorrow with it"* (paraphrased from Proverbs 10:26).

The second thing to remember is this. **The only way you can lose is if you quit!** No matter how overwhelming your circumstance may seem, you are not the first, nor are you the only human to experience such a thing. There are many people out there who have either been through it, or something very similar to it, and still emerged on top. As human beings, we are all made with the same basic programming. So, if they can do it, you can too. God made a way for you to endure the most formidable challenges with each other and still grow stronger through the process. In Christ, **there is always hope**.

So here we are in these crazy times with all of this Kingdom work to do... important work like winning the world for Jesus, defending the innocent, and feeding the poor. Sometimes it feels like we'll never be able to get it done. Yet, in the middle of all this activity, Holy Spirit is quietly leading us back to the basics of living healthier lifestyles; spirit, soul, and body. He is also leading us back to the basics of keeping a healthy marriage, His original design for filling the earth with His life and love.

It was God who created everything. It was God who designed the way it is supposed to work. He is the one with absolute truth to offer. He made us, wired us, and then equipped us with the most potent force this world has ever seen. A force so strong that even He, the very God who introduced it, couldn't say no to it. It caused Him to lay His very own life down for the ones He loves, His bride.

It may be the anointing that breaks the yolk of bondage, but passion pulls the plow.

Passion is the power of God that binds you to the heart of your spouse. Passion is the driving force that feeds and fosters your love for each other, fights for you, and protects you from the divisive attacks of the devil. Passion is what compels you to go beyond yourself, wrap your arms around each other and never, never, never let go. Passion sets you in your day and works perfect love through you that looks beyond the multitude of sins. Passionate love is what binds you together and makes you one.

Passion made this happen: *"So God created man in His own image; in the image of God He created him; male and female He created them. Then God blessed them, and God said to them, 'Be fruitful and multiply; fill the earth and subdue it; have dominion ...'"* (Genesis 1:27-28).

Because of passion, the very first thing God gave to man was each other!

Again, I don't claim to have all the answers you need, or that one magical elixir to fix all the problems you might face in your marriages. I don't know what each of your individual situations are, but I'm sure there are plenty of you facing genuine and legitimate challenges.

In that, there is one thing I do know. Whatever situation you face, God knew all about it. He's known since before the foundations of this earth were laid and therefore prepared you for it from the very beginning. He formed you, breathed His life into you, and equipped you both to subdue life... together as one!

So I have to ask. In these challenges you face in your life and marriage, could it be possible that maybe, just maybe, the solutions to your problems aren't quite as complicated as they may seem? Could it be that these relational challenges are not being caused nearly as much by the elements that are, but by the elements that are not? Could it be that your solution is as simple as a missing ingredient, a secret spice you've been needing but haven't been able to identify? Well, there is something I know that will spice up your marriage and fill it with fire and purpose... and it has been there all along. There is something I know that might be just what you are looking for. It may not fix every little thing that is broken, but if you are searching for a way to energize your marriage, to ensure it will last forever, or to set your hearts ablaze so they never stop burning for each other, I give you my story... Of Love and Bubbles.

God bless you and keep you, and make His face to shine upon you. I pray and declare Psalm 91 over every husband and wife relationship who reads this book. Go, stoke the fires and let your hearts burn with passion for each other ...

Go, make love happen!

DARES OLSON

As the author of this book, please allow me to introduce myself.

My name is Dares Olson, and I like long walks in the park (with my wife, of course).

I am an ordained minister from the Midwest who was raised in the home of an ordained minister. As a result, I have been involved in some form of ministry for most of my life. Over these years, the Holy Spirit has given me the ability to take tough topics that can be pretty complex or involved and explain them in a very real way that is not only understandable but relevant to our lives. I'm that guy whose message sometimes sounds lighthearted and straightforward but carries great depth.

When I finished writing this book, my wife and I had been married for 38 years and were still going strong. We have four children and several little spoilers (grandchildren) running around.

If you have any questions or comments, you can contact me at: https://linktr.ee/dares.connection.ministries

www.ingramcontent.com/pod-product-compliance
Lightning Source LLC
Chambersburg PA
CBHW011219120626
46545CB00010B/3069